I AM TAMAR
Come out of Hiding

Dr. Charlene D. Winley

DEDICATION

This book is dedicated to Tamar, whose incestuous rape stole her identity, thus preventing her from becoming a Queen.

Thousands of years later, millions of women like you experienced a traumatic event, thus changing the trajectory of their life.

Tamar, you are not alone.

We link together, lighting the way, carrying the scepter, and adjusting our crowns.

We vow to come out of hiding and tell our story so that you, too, can be healed.

It's time!

CONTENTS

Foreword i
Dr. Linda Harvey

1 **HISTORICAL BACKGROUND** 1
Dr. Charlene D. Winley

2 **PRESERVED FOR A TIME AS THIS** Pg # 17
Letitia Council

3 **I ONCE WAS LOST** Pg # 27
Natalia Duran

4 **SOMEONE'S IN MY GARDEN** Pg # 37
Dr. Linda Harvey

5 **GOD HAS SET ME FREE** Pg # 48
Sonya Anissa

6 **FROM SILENCED TO SILENCER** Pg # 57
Maia Johnson

7 **HEALED TO BE MADE WHOLE** Pg # 70
Natasha Jones

8 **BREAK A LEG** Pg # 81
Mia Overton-Smith

9 **BETRAYAL OF MY INNOCENCE** Pg # 94
Yvonnya Peoples

10 **CHOSEN** Pg # 105
Lana Short

11 **I AM MELODY** Pg # 112
Melody Sidberry

12 **TRAUMA TO TRIUMPH** Pg # 122
Roz Caldwell Stanley

13 **SMALL BENEFITS BIG PACKAGE** Pg # 135
Gloria J. Winley

14 **AFTERMATH** Pg # 146
Dr. Charlene D. Winley

I AM TAMAR

FOREWORD
Dr. Linda Harvey

I remember that day perfectly well. I stood at the corner, near the kitchen window, squinting my eyes as rays of sunshine warmed my cheeks. I remember the delightful scent of honeysuckles from the nearby shrub that gently perfumed the air. I can still remember how giddy I felt as I couldn't wait to go outside to pick a flower and carefully pull the long green stem that had just a few drops of nectar to taste. My mother was busy packing lunches, while I got dressed for school, adorning myself with that famous school uniform, a white blouse and pleated blue skirt, knee high socks with black and white shoes. I was very fond of school and enjoyed waiting at the bus stop with my friends. During the ride, we talked, laughed, and sang Ms. Mary Mack more times than I can count. As a young girl, budding into my pre-teen years, life was good. I felt safe, loved, and supported by my parents and family. Even the community we grew up in made me feel safe, everyone looked out for each other; especially the kids. But just as the season changed, so did my life.

The days of childhood bliss ended abruptly one dreadful day while riding the school bus. This is the day that he entered my life and completely ruined it. I can never forget how at that very moment I realized that the space was not enough for both of us to sit in as he pressed close to me. I cringed and almost curled into myself as he smiled with that dirty curled lip. My youthful singing lost its rhythm that day, and the sun hid its face in protest and a strange wind embraced my cheeks. That day, he broke my strand; my innocence and I desperately tried to pick up the pearls so no one would see my shame. It was that day, the day he bruised my blossom.

A jubilant soul now silenced, shamed by the deed he did until the bus route changed. His threats caused me to freeze and when I opened my month, there was no sound. I kept the secret year after year, pushing the memory back, like so many touched by sexual trauma. I was afraid, embarrassed, and always felt ugly and dirty. I hid that broken bruised girl in the recesses of my mind and tried to move on with my life. But that disaster changed my perception of life, I no longer felt good or safe. Muted. Confused. Scarred. How I longed for the days of sweet nectar from the Honeysuckle shrub and the cheerful songs I'd sing with my friends. I had to keep living and life continued with school graduations, birthdays, family vacations, even modeling and other special occasions.

The shadows of the past taunted me while relationships with beau's were hindered by my hidden wounds. Mood swings were constant and the cloak of shame, a regular garment. Anything and everything poised as a "trigger" and overtime, my excuses and hiding place shrank. My soul screamed over and over, you must tell, you must tell your story.

In October 2015, I sat with seven other women in a pilot group with House of Ruth (Maryland) and we learned how to tell our story. We cried for hours but did the work to become the 1st Graduate Storytellers now equipped to help others break the silence of sexual trauma.

I Am Tamar; a timely collaborative book written by Dr. Charlene Winley and other gifted authors is the "balm" needed in 2023. Current U.S. statistical data report that 1 out of 3 women will experience sexual trauma in her lifetime. Sexual trauma is a global epidemic and impacts girls younger than 3 years of age and women over 90. The world is filled with Tamars that have been bruised and shamed by persons who are familiar to them and strangers. Historically, many cultural and ethnic groups have taught girls not to tell to avoid family shaming, loss of funds by the provider/predator and other types of juridical punishment. Girls in rural counties are victimized daily and some are eventually forced to marry their abuser – this must end!

This timely book is so desperately needed in the hands of every girl and women. This book will become the catalyst providing a new awakening prompting strength, courage and giving the survivor a voice. We can no longer allow another generation of girls to suffer heinous acts of sexual trauma that's excused by a nod or a wink. I strongly feel this book will revolutionize a new consciousness breaking the fetters of shame for those yet in hiding. It's time to reintroduce Tamar. If that's you my sister, it's time to come out of hiding and tell your story. No more hiding, please find the strength to tell your story. My name is Linda, I Am Tamar.

1

HISTORICAL BACKGROUND
Dr. Charlene D Winley

Why I am Writing This Book

Although it's been over ten years since I started writing this book, it was born out of a dramatization that I was scheduled to perform at a friend's conference. In preparation for this conference, I labored before the Lord for two weeks on what He wanted to impart to the women regarding the incestuous rape of Tamar. It was of utmost importance that Holy Spirit ministered to and through me to speak to the hearts of the women in the audience. The event took place, Holy Spirit led another way, and I did not release what was birth in me until now.

The name "The Tamar Project" was given two days before the would-be conference. I thought it was going to be the name of my new ministry or a non-profit organization. I was oblivious that the many nights and early morning wake-ups of writing, reading, and rewriting were preparing me for the daunting task ahead.

When you open this book, you will walk the path of the silent majority… a small number representing many who experienced the violent assault of physical, emotional, or sexual abuse. Some stories are very graphic and painful to read. We all agreed to open our lives and share our process. All the women tell their stories in the first person and are all called Tamar. I thought the name Tamar was appropriate because she was a princess, a victim of incest, violated, and abused by her half-brother, Amnon, ignored by her father and King, David, and hushed by her brother, Absalom.

My name is Charlene, and I make no claims of being an expert on rape, sexual abuse, or molestation. I can only share my journey and process as a former victim, now a victor of sexual abuse. I trust that my coming out of the darkness will give a voice to those caught in the aftermath of their storms.

So, come forth and begin the healing process.

Proverbs 25:4 *"Take away the dross from the silver, and there shall come forth a vessel for the finer."* KJV

I say begin because recovery from abuse is a lifelong process. Transformation involves relearning, undoing mindsets, overcoming strongholds, and being Rescripted. Although it does not take a lifetime for Holy Spirit to do His work, it can take a lifetime for abuse victims to recover their souls and regain their identity. From the moment of the assault, you took on a new identity and developed a new belief system and ideologies, subsequently changing your life trajectory. Everything you came to believe, how you react, your very nature and your personality became skewed by that one, or in some cases, years of repeated violent acts against your soul. Your soul is where your heart, will, and emotions are seated. Even years after the abuse, patterns of behaviors are imprinted in your psyche to the point that you can no longer recall your behaviors before the abuse. For those taking on the task of recovery, it is a lifelong process of transforming and renewing the mind and loving yourself again.

Romans 12:1-2 (AMP)

1 I appeal to you therefore, brethren, and beg of you in view of [all] the mercies of God, to make a decisive dedication of your bodies [presenting all your members and faculties] as a living sacrifice, holy (devoted, consecrated) and well pleasing to God, which is your reasonable (rational, intelligent) service and

spiritual worship.
2 Do not be conformed to this world (this age), [fashioned after
and adapted to its external, superficial customs], but be
transformed (changed) by the [entire] renewal of your mind [by its
new ideals and its new attitude], so that you may prove [for
yourselves] what is the good and acceptable and perfect will of
God, even the thing which is good and acceptable and perfect [in
His sight for you].

When I started writing this book in 2010, another area of healing was uncovered for me. I would have described myself as an "I can DO-IT-ALL BY MYSELF" woman at that time. You name it, I can do it. I learned to be strong, self-reliant, dependent, tenacious, and resourceful. I no longer worry about being hurt or disappointed because instead of relying on others to do it incorrectly, fall short, or not attempt the assignment…hey, you can rest assured I will get it done. And in some cases, ALL BY MYSELF. I learned to keep people at bay, arm's distance away, so they did not get too close and ever hurt or disappoint me again." WHY??? Because it was those closest to me that tore a hole in my soul.

This revelation was shocking to me. I read the book, *Boundaries-When to Protect Yourself* by Henry McCloud and Robert Townsend. I understood the disparity between boundaries and walls. They were clear. Boundaries let the good flow in and short-circuit negativity by keeping it out. On the other hand, walls keep everything, the good, bad, and indifferent.....OUT. I worked on myself in my self-prescribed therapy sessions, journaled, cried too many tears, and was tormented by too many dreams, only to face the reality of something else still lurking in my soul.

Once again. Really God, I thought everything was made anew. Another layer of skin to peel back. I cried out to my Father for cleansing, healing, and restoration. Why must the pain go so deep into my core? When is it going to end? On the outside, I looked great (but there were days when even that was questionable).

One day amid one of my pity parties, Holy Spirit said, "Isolation and independence! This must not be. For I created you for relationship." I was unaware of my actions and the distance I created between myself and others. I never knew; I never made lasting connections with folks. It was far easier to keep people at a safe distance. This was one of the reasons why it was so easy for me to get up and relocate to another state so quickly without ever looking back. Over the past 22 years in Virginia Beach, I cried enough tears to fill a river. I felt like a hopeless failure and thought

I would never climb out of my pit of despair. I have been made whole through my process of healing and ReScripting my life.

The Sins of the Father

King David had eight named wives, others unnamed, and countless concubines. He fathered nineteen sons and one daughter, the royal princess Tamar.

Tamar and Absalom were the children of David and Maacah, the daughter of Talmai, King of Geshur. According to the author, Tamar Kidari, in the account, *"Maacah the wife of David: Midrash and Aggadah." Jewish Women: A Comprehensive Historical Encyclopedia,* "David saw Maacah when he went forth to war; he desired her, and he took her as an *eshet yefat to'ar,* a non-Jewish woman taken captive during wartime and who is desired by her Israelite captor, who wants to marry her. He may do so under the conditions specified in Deuteronomy 21:10–14." Jacob Bernstein further describes this account in the article "Eshet Yefat To'ar: A New Look" as follows.

> After victory in battle, a group of soldiers passes some locals, and one woman catches a certain sergeant's eye. He separates from his fellow troops to gaze at her outstanding beauty and decides to approach her. Before she is able to react, he forces her into an alleyway and fulfills his war-

driven sexual cravings. Subsequently, he travels back to his native country with her at his side and proceeds to shave off her hair, grow her fingernails beyond their normal length, strip away her beautiful clothing, and dress her in sackcloth. He lives out his daily life, returning to his family and friends whom he left for war, while his normal surroundings embrace an additional character: his captive. After thirty days, he forcibly converts her to his religion and marries her. Bernstein, 2012

During this time, the woman mourns for her family. After being brutally raped, she was kidnapped and taken as a wife by the enemy. According to Bernstein, 2012, "The poor woman's life has been ruined, and, beyond the abuse and assault, she has now been transformed into a new person, implanted into new faith, family, and surroundings." Bernstein, 2012. As we read the Biblical account, David's sons, Amnon and Absalom, later perpetuate this violent act.

According to the author, "Rabbis frowned on the practice of marrying two wives" because one is usually loved while the other is hated; The practice of disfiguring a woman was to make her unattractive to her captor. This trickled down in how the children of Maacah, the eshet yefat to'ar, were treated and behaved. This brought dissension in David's household, and as we

I AM TAMAR

will later see, Absalom revolted against his father and tried to overthrow his throne. This is a pause for thought. I often wonder if Tamar's mother's status weighed heavily on David's decision, both as a father and king, to ignore the incestuous rape and not to defend Tamar's honor. He did not love her, Maacah, and perhaps he did not love Tamar.

This act would later prove disastrous as Amnon was assassinated by Absalom's servants two years later. In total, Absalom silenced his sister, Tamar, slept with his father's wives in broad daylight, caused dissension in Israel, and was responsible for the deaths of Shimei, son of Gera, Sheba, son of Bichri, Ahithophel, Mephibosheth, and Ish-bosheth.

This generational curse of lust and murder was passed from David to his sons. David's desire for women, specifically Bathsheba and Maacah (he had seven wives), was passed through his loins to his sons, Amnon, Absalom, and Solomon.

Tamar's Story

2 Samuel 13:1-22   The Message (MSG)

13 1-4 *Some time later, this happened: Absalom, David's son, had a sister who was very attractive. Her name was Tamar. Amnon, also David's son, was in love with her. Amnon was obsessed with*

8

his sister Tamar to the point of making himself sick over her. She was a virgin, so he couldn't see how he could get his hands on her. Amnon had a good friend, Jonadab, the son of David's brother Shimeah. Jonadab was exceptionally streetwise. He said to Amnon, "Why are you moping around like this, day after day—you, the son of the king! Tell me what's eating at you."

"In a word, Tamar," said Amnon. "My brother Absalom's sister. I'm in love with her."

5 "Here's what you do," said Jonadab. "Go to bed and pretend you're sick. When your father comes to visit you, say, 'Have my sister Tamar come and prepare some supper for me here where I can watch her and she can feed me.'"

6 So Amnon took to his bed and acted sick. When the king came to visit, Amnon said, "Would you do me a favor? Have my sister Tamar come and make some nourishing dumplings here where I can watch her and be fed by her."

7 David sent word to Tamar who was home at the time: "Go to the house of your brother Amnon and prepare a meal for him."

8-9 So Tamar went to her brother Amnon's house. She took dough, kneaded it, formed it into dumplings, and cooked them while he watched from his bed. But when she took the cooking pot and served him, he wouldn't eat.

9-11 Amnon said, "Clear everyone out of the house," and they all cleared out. Then he said to Tamar, "Bring the food into my bedroom, where we can eat in privacy." She took the nourishing dumplings she had prepared and brought them to her brother Amnon in his bedroom. But when she got ready to feed him, he grabbed her and said, "Come to bed with me, sister!"

12-13 "No, brother!" she said, "Don't hurt me! This kind of thing isn't done in Israel! Don't do this terrible thing! Where could I ever show my face? And you—you'll be out on the street in disgrace. Oh, please! Speak to the king—he'll let you marry me."

14 But he wouldn't listen. Being much stronger than she, he raped her.

15 No sooner had Amnon raped her than he hated her—an immense hatred. The hatred that he felt for her was greater than the love he'd had for her. "Get up," he said, "and get out!"

16-18 "Oh no, brother," she said. "Please! This is an even worse evil than what you just did to me!"

9

*But he wouldn't listen to her. He called for his valet. "Get rid of this woman. Get her out of my sight! And lock the door after her."
The valet threw her out and locked the door behind her.*
18-19 *She was wearing a long-sleeved gown. (That's how virgin princesses used to dress from early adolescence on.) Tamar poured ashes on her head, then she ripped the long-sleeved gown, held her head in her hands, and walked away, sobbing as she went.*
20 *Her brother Absalom said to her, "Has your brother Amnon had his way with you? Now, my dear sister, let's keep it quiet—a family matter. He is, after all, your brother. Don't take this so hard." Tamar lived in her brother Absalom's home, bitter and desolate.*
21-22 *King David heard the whole story and was enraged, but he didn't discipline Amnon. David doted on him because he was his firstborn. Absalom quit speaking to Amnon—not a word, whether good or bad—because he hated him for violating his sister Tamar."*

The Victimization of Tamar

Amnon- the name means "faithful." He is King's David firstborn son and half-brother of Tamar and Absalom.
Absalom-the name means, "My Father is peace." He is David's third-born son and brother of Tamar.
Tamar-the name means "palm tree." She is King David's daughter and sister of Absalom. E. Fletcher

David had 19 sons and one daughter, Tamar, and this is her story.

Tamar's Position

Tamar was a royal princess. Her mother, Maacah, also born of royalty, was King Talmi of Geshur's daughter from the neighboring country of Geshur. As the daughter of King David and as a royal princess, she was a royal virgin kept under close guard. She was never to go outside the walls unguarded or alone.

Therefore, she was out of Amnon's reach. Tamar is a woman of

very high moral standards and is described as having only sisterly

love for him.

> Tamar was confined by court protocol to the women's
> quarters and guarded there by the eunuchs attached to
> David's harem, so getting her alone was no easy matter.
> But Amnon and his cousin, Jonadab, invented a ruse to lure
> her into Amnon's bedroom. Elizabeth Fletcher

Tamar was strikingly beautiful, and Amnon, her half-brother, was

so in love with her that he made himself sick. He could never

marry his half-sister because Jewish laws forbid sexual relations

between siblings. Read Leviticus 18:9, 11, 20:17 KJV, and

Deuteronomy 27:22 KJV. Tamar would have had a marriage

arranged for her when she was still a child. This was the usual

procedure for royal princesses. Like most royal weddings, the

young man would have been a prince from a neighboring country.

Tamar's marriage would have been used to cement relations with

King David's emerging kingdom of Israel, expanding his territory

and strengthening his alliances. But things did not go as planned.

Amnon was David's firstborn child, and he was privileged

and did not know how to deal with the fact that he wanted his

sister, Tamar, and she was not feeling the same way. As he began to pour out his heart to his cousin, Jonadab, an evil plan was conceived to get Tamar within arm's reach of her brother, Amnon. I often wonder what was lurking in Jonadab's spirit that even he would conceive such an atrocity against his cousin, Tamar. Jonadab will later team up with Absalom and set up Amnon to be murdered.

Amnon wanted what he wanted, and he was all in with the scheme to rape Tamar as his lust and obsession for her grew out of control. Amnon faked an illness and called for his father, King David. King David arrived and wanted to see his first-born son fully recover as soon as possible. The fact that Amnon was sick to the point of not eating was disconcerting to King David. He had difficulty saying "No," to his children, especially Amnon, and usually gave them everything they wanted. Amnon knowing this, asked his father, "I pray thee, let my sister, Tamar, come and make me a couple of cakes in my sight, that I may eat from her hand." 2 Samuel 13: 6b, KJV

The Assault

King David told his daughter, Tamar, to go immediately to her brother Amnon's place and cook for him. King David, Tamar's father, provider, and protector, disregards, or has a lapse in judgment, or forgets that he, too, "watched" Bathsheba and desired Maacah and puts his daughter in harm's way. Obedient to her father, Tamar does as requested. She leaves her place of safety, and she cooks for her brother. Tamar was obedient to her father and king, and although she may have had reservations about going to her brother's private quarters, she was ordered to do so by her father. Tamar brings the food to her brother, Amnon, and puts it in the area outside the bedroom chamber. He orders her to bring it to the room because he is ill. She obeys and sets it before him. He refuses to eat and is still faking his sickness; he needs to be hand fed by his sister. What other way would he get her close enough? He orders everyone out, leaving him and Tamar alone. She is unaware of the trap that will forever change the course of her life and hurl her into history as the first account of the incestuous rape of a royal princess in the Bible.

Remember the account of David and Macccah? Tamar's mother he took captive as his eshet yefat to'ar during wartime? This same incident is repeated between Tamar and Amnon, as he desires his half-sister and forces himself on her. Rape violates and

13

throws her away. Once finished with the brutal rape, Amnon's hate

for Tamar was more potent than his love for her. He ordered her

out. She refused to go and asked that he marry her. He had his

guard forcibly removed from his private court and locked the door.

Tamar was now dishonored and ripped her royal robe of

many colors. The royal robe set her apart from the other women in

the court, because it was worn exclusively by royal princesses. As

a sign of distress, she places ashes on her head and cries out.

As she staggered toward the harem quarters, she cried out

loud and into her mother's arms. Quickly, the women surmised

what took place and the harem was in a uproar. The lives of three

women intertwined forever in history, as they would be the most

affected, Tamar, her mother, Maacah, and Ahinoam, the mother of

Amnon.

Her brother, Absalom, told her, "He's your brother, do not

take it to heart." Was it possible that Absalom already had a plan in

mind? King David is confronted by Tamar's mother, Maacah, and

brother, Absalom. He is devastated yet does not chastise or punish

his first-born son, Amnon, whom he loves dearly. He could have

forced them to marry to maintain Tamar's dignity. Still, then they could never have sexual relations even as a married couple because was forbidden in Israel, sexual relations between siblings. He could have exiled or excommunicated Amnon from his kingdom, but He did not. We see here that David failed Tamar as a father for not punishing Amnon as a son and failed as a king for not punishing him as a criminal.

Tamar's life was now ruined. Without the forbidden marriage to her half-brother, Amnon, she would forever remain unmarried, childless, and unable to fulfill her role as a queen. She would never be accepted as a wife by another man, and Tamar would be condemned to spending the rest of her life in the back room of the harem.

Without the edict of the king punishing Amnon and doing something, everyone else was powerless to come to the aid of Tamar. Like many women today, the abuser is protected, and the victim is vilified. She becomes silenced and ignored, and the crime is never spoken of again. This decision determines the fate of her position as a royal princess. She would be a little higher than a servant.

Remember Absalom? He was not forgiving and would seek

revenge, as vendetta was part of Near Eastern culture. Many historians believe that Amnon knew he wouldn't be King or next to the throne because Absalom's mother, Maacah, was of royal birth and held the highest status of King David's wives. Maybe Amnon was not only obsessed, but he was jealous of their beauty and position. This could have been his way of bringing sin and reproach to Maacah's lineage. Absalom vowed to avenge the rape of his sister, Tamar. The prophetic word that Nathan spoke was in motion. Absalom waited for the opportunity to strike and kill his half-brother, Amnon.

2 Samuel 12:10-12 KJV

*"**10** Now therefore the sword shall never depart from thine house; because thou hast despised me, and hast taken the wife of Uriah the Hittite to be thy wife.*
__11__ Thus saith the Lord, Behold, I will raise up evil against thee out of thine own house, and I will take thy wives before thine eyes, and give them unto thy neighbour, and he shall lie with thy wives in the sight of this sun.
__12__ For thou didst it secretly: but I will do this thing before all Israel, and before the sun.
Did the murder of Amnon help Tamar in any way? Probably not. It may have given her some fleeting satisfaction, but as matters stood, she was condemned to the life of a childless widow."

2

PRESERVED FOR A TIME AS THIS
Letitia Council

"Walk with me, Lord, walk with me. While I'm on my pilgrim's journey, I want Jesus to walk with me."
(UMC Discipleship)

I recall being fearful of sharing my story of tragedy; though I wasn't the one who was physically injured, I knew I was impacted. My heart had a lot to say, a cry to speak, but every time I was alone, I heard a voice saying, "No one cares about your impact and how the tragedy affected you." The mistake was allowing that voice to shut me up. For months, I let that voice continue to silence me before I could share with people and speak about the tragedy that shooked my life. That voice was the voice of fear, trying to keep my mouth closed and silence me from speaking. I have allowed fear the authority at times to keep me silent. Each morning, I would wake up knowing my life had been changed, and yet, I would push through the day, accepting my new norm while allowing fear to control me. Those who knew of the tragedy which occurred on the evening of August 15, 2019, prayed for my daughter and our family. That night, my oldest daughter, Ja' Nasia, was in a motor vehicle accident that caused life-threatening injuries. She had to be cut out of the car after it flipped twice, hitting a tree and a utility box Southbound on 64 in Chesapeake, Virginia. That night Ja'Nasia sustained a right frontal hematoma to her head, went unconscious, and was placed on a ventilator, which caused her to be diagnosed with a Traumatic Brain Injury. I can never really put in writing how I felt that night. All I can remember is that I didn't want to lose my precious daughter, and the doctor said she had just a little time to live, but God said, "Not So!" After undergoing brain surgery, a gastrointestinal tracheotomy, and a tracheotomy placed, my daughter was released 28 days later to rehab. Ja'Nasia stayed in rehabilitation for three weeks to the date of her admission and was finally able to return home for the first time since walking out the door the evening of the accident. After all our family had been through, the weight on my shoulders as a mother and wife, the fear of speaking about our daughter's death was still there but not as visible.

In January 2020, God spoke to me and gave me "The Nasia Foundation" and said, "You will assist other moms with teens who have become affected by Traumatic Brain Injury and raise awareness throughout the region and nation." I had no idea what that meant or how I would pull through, but I trusted God and His plan, and with uncertainty, I did what God instructed me to do. In April 2020, I did the paperwork to start a nonprofit organization. Within two weeks, our approval letter came in the mail. Since then, we have been breaking the chain of fear and silence within the Brain Injury Community. Many felt hope was lost, and many were afraid to speak out. A brain injury will cause survivors to become stuck in the "silent epidemic." As a caregiver, I was too silent in fear about sharing my story. Why was I falling into that trap when I knew that God had entrusted me to be the voice to break the silence of fear? It was "me" standing in the way of "me." By the end of 2020, I had begun to speak out about my story, and fear began to shed. I had built up the confidence to trust the women God had assigned to me to help push me out of fear, silence, and rejection. The more I stayed connected, the more fear was shedding. God said, "The last shall be first, and the first shall be last. I have not forgotten or overlooked you."

In March of 2021, I was on fire!!! I would encourage myself and prepare for weekly educational Facebook Lives, raising awareness about Traumatic Brain Injury and how it affected my life. I had begun to do what God expected me to do with my assignment. I was like, "God, this is good. You are assisting me in helping those in need and empowering them from what could have taken them out. God, if you kept my mind throughout my trauma, I know you will keep their minds." I was giving words of encouragement, sending out inspirational care boxes, and starting to encourage myself. A year had passed since the accident, and my daughter's prognosis was improving. She began moving her mouth and doing other activities involving her limbs. "God, I thank you that every day wasn't the same." A resolve was ignited in Nasia, and she was approved for a communication device in which she would use her eyes to communicate. God was blowing our minds daily. My relationship with God had grown stronger within a year. We were still in the middle of the COVID pandemic, but God was still working on our behalf. I didn't let fear take me out. I was moving forward. I spoke to the fear and let it know that it was time to go, and I was coming out of agreement with every thought that held me, hostage. Fear, rejection, and anxiety had to go. God was preparing me for what was yet to come, and all I could do was Trust Him.

On April 25, 2021, God did what He knew was best, yet I couldn't believe I had to face the reality of what had just occurred. God called my daughter, Ja'Nasia, home to her resting place, and Nasia answered. My heart wasn't ready. He tried to prepare me by showing me numerous visions I shook off because I didn't want to see, believe, or accept them. God showed me two visions; the first was my cell phone ringing while I was at church, and the screen showed "Hubby." My husband and I stood over an empty casket in the second vision. The sign in front of the casket read, "The New City" (our church's name). Both times, I shook the images. Two months before the visions, God had shown me the number 25. On April 25, my daughter said, "Mommy, I'm okay." While crying on my front porch, God revealed why He gave me the number 25 and why I knew there would be a 911 call that day.

God called my daughter home eight days after my thirty-eighth birthday. Two days before He called her, He answered my prayers that I had been praying for since August 15, 2019. I told God that I wanted to hear my daughter's voice. I hadn't heard her speak since that day when she called me ten minutes before the accident occurred. God listened and responded to a mother's prayer; Nasia said, "Mom." God had given me the supernatural strength to plan my daughter's homegoing celebration with my husband right by my side. My husband was the one who found our daughter unresponsive. He called me on the phone, trying to hide the fear in his heart of what the reality was. When I arrived home, fear gripped my heart. I wasn't ready for what was yet to come. I thought my daughter would be rushed to the hospital for some unexpected symptoms from her injury. But the reality was our daughter had passed away in our home. Fear of how I would live without her played over and over in my mind. Truth is, I never imagined life without my beautiful daughter. I was supposed to leave this earth before her, not her leave before me. I had adapted to how my life had altered on the evening of the accident, but now I had to adjust and cope all over again.

Fear is a mind thing; if we train our minds to release, let go, and let God, we shall overcome it. Yes, I overcame it, but I had to be willing to walk through it. It took some time. My family and I began to truly feel grief's effects as we started planning for the funeral. Grief is an experience that has no expiration date. Although there is a process that you go through to learn to cope without your child physically being here on earth, the sorrow and grief never die. My mind was made up not to allow grief to consume me, I knew God had so much planned for me, but I also knew I couldn't rush back into the community. The hardest part of the grieving process was letting go and seeking counseling. It was hard for me to let go of the fact my daughter was no longer alive. I didn't want to seek counseling. God told me I needed to, and I told God I didn't need counseling, "I'm okay."

About two weeks later, I had my second breakdown. I told God I was sorry because who was I to tell Him what I didn't need? Once my counseling sessions began, I could release the grief and the pain of sorrow. I began to feel so much better. My therapist reminded me that letting go of grief isn't letting go of the memories of my daughter, and I feared letting go of grief because of that. Once I began to heal from the most challenging part of grief, I could breathe without suffocating under fear... yea, fear had to go.

After six months of counseling, God spoke to me and said, "It's time to come out of Hiding." I began to *rise up from the ashes of my trauma*. Chains were broken, and all fear was gone. The memories of my daughter were for a lifetime, and grief could no longer hold me bound. God gave me a vision; I wrote it down, and within five months, it was executed. The Women on the Move Conference was birthed. The first conference was held and subtitled "Rising from the Ashes of HER Trauma." God handpicked each woman, and He also moved mighty during the event. He said he would blow my mind.

Next, I became a best-selling author for the third time. In December 2022, I launched my first solo project, "Hope for Grieving Mothers-12-Day Devotional Journal for Grieving Mothers." When God says, 'Move and come out of hiding,' He means, "Trust me, daughter, with your whole life, I have you, I will be with you wherever you go, and you shall not fail."

Proverbs 46:5 "God is within her; she will not fall God will help her at break of day. NIV
Proverbs 3:5-6 "Trust in the Lord with all thine heart; and lean

not unto thine own understanding. In all thy ways acknowledge him, and he shall direct thy paths." KJV

Trusting God is one of the best decisions I have ever made. I didn't throw in the towel like my flesh wanted to. My organization, The Nasia Foundation, is thriving, and my new business, Letitia Council, LLC, was just birthed. I have come out of hiding, and I am now ready for my Godly assignment to assist women to rise from the ashes of their trauma and coach them to be the beautiful butterfly mothers they have grown to be.

I am Tamar, and this is my story!

I want Jesus to walk with me. Retrieved May 13, 2023, from https://christianmusicandhymns.com/2022/10/i-want-jesus-to-walk-with-me.html

BIOGRAPHY
Letitia Council

Four-time #1 Amazon Bestselling Author, Inspirational Speaker, Certified Life Coach, Certified Christian Mental Health Specialist, and Non-Profit Founder. Inspired by a genuine desire to help others, Letitia Council, Founder, and President of The Nasia Foundation, is a woman on a mission. She is a Traumatic Brain Injury & Caregiver Advocate who loves to share her story about her WHY? She encourages women and assists them in rising from the ashes of their trauma. She has been blessed to be a part of many different organizations that support those in need. Letitia is a published author and has been a part of four anthologies. She is currently part of two anthologies, *I am Tamar-Come out of Hiding and Heeled: Walking from Pain to Purpose in God.* She has an Associate of Occupational Science Degree in Medical Assisting from Tidewater Tech. She has been featured on the Power and Grace Leaders Talk Show, BIG Mind Entertainment Real Notes Talk Show, Coast Live Show, and Voyage ATL Magazine. Letitia is the founder of Women on the Move Conference and Butterfly Moms Support Group. She is the owner of Letitia Council, LLC. Letitia is a loving, caring, devoted wife of 11 years to her amazingly supportive husband. She is a mother of five children, and their oldest daughter Ja'Nasia Miller, Traumatic Brain Injury Angel, transitioned on April 25, 2021. She now calls herself a Butterfly Mom.

Facebook-Letitia Council
Instagram-Letitia Council
LinkedIn- Letitia Council

3

I ONCE WAS LOST
Natalia Duran

It was a cool spring day in the beautiful state of Utah. Birds were chirping, bees were buzzing, and you could see children from all over the neighborhood playing amidst sounds of laughter. As a child, I should be doing what other children did, like riding bikes and jumping jump ropes, but that wasn't the case. I was playing in the field of my country home with an empty beer bottle that belonged to my stepfather in one hand and collecting his half-smoked cigarettes with the other. It was 1991, and I was only five years of age when I began attempting to smoke the cigarettes I found throughout our yard. My sibling and I would hide behind an old shed in the backyard and light the cigarettes we had collected in our empty beer bottles.

During that same year, I was riding around with my stepfather as he sipped on his favorite beer and did donuts in the parking lot full of snow and ice, an activity we did regularly. I would frequently ask my stepfather why I was not allowed to drink beer. As a young child, I did not understand why I could not drink the same thing I observed him drinking from the time he woke up until he went to bed. However, this day was different; he let me try the beer for the very first time. He laughed hysterically as my sibling tried it first and then spat it out everywhere. When it was my turn, my response differed from my siblings. The moment I took the first sip of alcohol, I did not spit it out or scream; rather, I asked him for more. That was the start of my tampering with cigarettes and alcohol. The spouts of "experimenting" continued from there on out until the age of 11. By that time, I was smoking cigarettes daily and drinking alcohol as frequently as I could without my parents finding out. Because there was an abundance of cigarettes and alcohol throughout our home, I could often steal both without my parents ever knowing. In addition, I hung out with people much older than me and with people whose parents would contribute to my addictive behavior; therefore, gaining access to substances at a young age was not problematic for me. Shortly after beginning to smoke cigarettes and drink alcohol, I also began smoking weed and taking hallucinates. I would spend time with older crowds, late nights, and weekends away from home doing whatever I wanted, which was frequent throughout my early teenage years.

My stepfather and biological father were both alcoholics, and most men I was surrounded with growing up were the same. My biological father was in and out of my life until age 11, when he chose to sign his rights over, and my stepfather adopted me. Physical, mental, and emotional abuse were all a part of my childhood. At the age of 10, I was sexually abused by a neighbor, and at the age of 15, still a virgin at the time, I was raped by a much older male friend. I moved out of my parent's house and dropped out of school around the time I was 15. In 2003, when I was just 17 years old, I met what I thought at the time to be the man of my dreams. He was fresh out of prison, 29 years old, covered in tattoos, and the leader of a gang in my city. I did not grow up knowing what a good man was, so the fact that a much older man expressed interest in me was greatly attractive. When he began giving me attention and making me feel loved, I thought it was everything that my father was not. I latched on to his charisma quickly. Shortly after getting together, I noticed his actions consistently differed from his words. I caught him in lies, found drugs in his possession, and gradually began to allow him to speak to me and treat me in a way I always swore that I would never tolerate from a man. Not long into our relationship, he ended up in prison for doing drugs while on parole, and I ended the relationship abruptly. After just 9 months in prison, he was released on parole again and quickly contacted me. I made excuses and justified previous behavior and reluctantly, yet willingly, entered back into the relationship. He kept asking me to marry him and would often express that the way he felt about me was a way he had never felt about anyone else. However, the lies and the way he treated me were inconsistent with what he said.

One evening before we married, I remember he got upset with me over something extremely minor. I turned around to walk away, and before I knew it, he grabbed a towel, wrapped it around my neck, and began choking me until I nearly passed out while shouting vulgar things at me and calling me names. Although he

30

had broken many of my things before this, spat on me, and even threw things at me, I had always dismissed the abuse and said, "He was not abusive because he did not actually hit me."

Immediately after the first episode of physical abuse, he began to excessively apologize and express that his actions resulted from me not being the woman I should be. He justified his abuse towards me by shaming me as a woman and making me feel guilty for not doing or being how he expected. His actions were everything I saw growing up, and the words that followed kept me in a cycle of believing I deserved the abuse just like I experienced as a child. I will never forget the battle in my head when he used a towel to choke me. I thought about a lot of things and wondered how he could do that to me. I'm sure he knew what he was doing and was wise enough to ensure no marks or proof of the abuse. However, the manipulating words spoken to me kept me in a place of shame and guilt, justifying his behavior and believing that I deserved it.

Although this was the first of many instances of physical abuse throughout our marriage, it was not the last. Each time the abusive episodes would get worse than the time before, and each time he would apologize, and I would believe I did something to deserve it. It was a vicious cycle of him abusing me and making me feel responsible for his behavior. The mind games that wrapped around the abuse were so intense that I often did not know the truth from a lie or reality from the stories I made up to protect and cover up what was happening in our relationship. As a result of all that was happening, an addiction to drugs began to grow immensely. I went from drinking and smoking weed to taking pills, and eventually, I started doing heroin and meth. It felt like I wanted to numb the pain with drugs and falsify reality more and more the higher I got. I lived a life full of abuse, pain, lying, cheating, and deceit. I was institutionalized several times, went to jail, attempted different rehabs, and eventually ended up homeless living on the streets. Busted and disgusted, none of my family spoke to me, and I had exhausted every friendship.

In 2012, a proclaimed atheist, I moved to Tulsa, Oklahoma, from Salt Lake City, Utah, to try and get clean from drugs. I worked at a local restaurant as a manager, and many of the employees there were all Christians who attended the same local church. I would see the life these Christians lived, and I desired it so much. However, the shame and guilt from my past made me believe that God would never receive me as His own. I would hear testimonies from people of what God brought them out of. They would tell me that we have all sinned and fallen short of His glory but that nothing I had done separated me from His love. They explained to me that when God sent His one and only son to die on the cross, it was not just for them but for me, too (Romans 3:23, Romans 8:38, John 3:16 KJV). Although many people would attempt to pour into me, I continued to believe that I had sinned too much and that my addiction was too deep for God to love me.

I returned to Utah in 2013 and ended up on drugs worse than I ever had been before. Although I had not previously given my life to the Lord, every time I got high or was in situations where I felt scared or alone, I would begin to meditate on the things the people back in Tulsa had spoken to me. My desire for my lifestyle began to decrease, and my curiosity about knowing if God was real was starting to increase. I would attend churches randomly, often high on drugs or drunk on alcohol. I would sit and watch and wonder if one day I would be able to have the things I saw the people in the churches with.

During my back and forth in churches, my mother gave her life to the Lord and started attending church. She and a group of believers began to pray for me. In December 2015, while living on the streets, my mother contacted me. She offered to help me get off the streets with an ultimatum attached. I was to attend Bible college or go into a rehab facility. I knew I did not want to see another rehab facility; therefore, I moved to Tulsa and started Bible college in January 2016. I only attended for six months, drank, and got high throughout my enrollment. However, the words I heard spoken to me in Tulsa, Oklahoma, continued to impact my desire for something different.

Finally, in 2017, I fully surrendered and gave my life to the Lord after a supernatural encounter with Him in the bedroom of my mother's home. I got water baptized, filled with the Holy Ghost, and was supernaturally delivered from the remaining drugs I was using. I was finally free from tobacco and alcohol. I have been fully clean and walking with the Lord since. I went through a process of renewing my mind and was rapidly transformed into a different person (Romans 12:2 KJV). I am now a mother, a mentor to individuals who have experienced similar traumas, an honorable daughter instead of an addicted one, an aunt, and a sister. I work a full-time job, am a part of multiple prayer teams, am trusted, do not lie or steal, live in a home and not on the streets, and drive around in a car instead of a bicycle or walking. But the most remarkable thing is that I am a daughter of a King, I am healed, and I am no longer hiding because of my past.

I am Tamar, and this is my story!

BIOGRAPHY
Natalia Duran

Natalia Duran grew up in Utah and now resides in Oklahoma. While growing up, she was involved in drugs, was physically and sexually abused, married a gang leader, and later ended up homeless, strung out on meth and heroin. In 2017, at 31, Natalia gave her life to the Lord and has since graduated from cosmetology school. She became a mother and foster mother and adopted a child. As a working mother, she serves at the church, is heavily involved on different prayer teams throughout her city, and mentor individuals to help them overcome childhood addiction and trauma. She has a passion for seeing people overcome past addictions and traumas. She has a passion for working with the youths helping them take preventative measures against the wrong path in life.

She has been featured on "Health Topics with Ernestine Hopkins," a podcast about healing and overcoming addiction. Natalia speaks at churches and youth groups in her community, serves in her church, Gates of Refuge, as an intercessor, and teaches the youth. She is an advocate for the lost and broken and desires to see people turn their lives around from a place of being lost to a place of having life through Jesus.

Ministry: Serve on a homeless ministry team at Mother Tucker Ministry

Facebook -Natalia Duran

4

SOMEONE'S IN MY GARDEN
Apostle Dr. Linda Harvey

Olde to the days of childhood when life was simple, carefree and secure. My morning, like most mornings, consisted of a variety showcase of popular cereals, Cream of Wheat, Quaker Oatmeal, or the anticipated snap-crackle and pop from a bowl of Kellogg's Rice Krispies. I could hear my mom pouring sugary sweet Sunny Delight into cups and placing cereal bowls on the table.

My siblings and I were dubbed by relatives, the Johnson Six, and being the oldest, that was not always humorous. With six school age kids in the house, life was pretty interesting. I knew that eventually, the morning routine would be passed to me as my parents thought I was maturing and able to handle the responsibilities. To anyone reading my chapter, and you happen to be the oldest, you understand what I mean. There was never any real volunteerism that I can recall, only gentle delegation.

Mom's bustling in the morning was the key to getting

ready! I could time myself down to the clanging sound of the last spoon. My hair was in a soft flip, and the basic school uniform-blue pleated skirt, white blouse, blue sweater, knee-high knee socks, and the popular footwear of my *day*, black and white saddle shoes. By the time Mom would say, "Breakfast is ready," I was already downstairs in the living room, standing in my favorite spot. Nearest to the kitchen was a window cradling the sun's rays. Taking those few moments to soak up the heavenly beam was comforting. I can't remember when I started this daily ritual, but it was important to me and quite soothing.

As the last snap-crackle and pop melody faded, we would grab our lunches and make haste for school. My younger siblings usually walked to the elementary school near our home while I waited with friends for the bus that transported us to another. There in the dew of the morning, we coordinated our hand clapping to the popular nursery rhyme, "Ms. Mary Mack." Of course, we enjoyed other sing-a-longs; sometimes, adding our verse that resulted in tearful laughter.

Those are the times I fondly remember; when the sun kissed my cheeks, and the fading taste of nectar from honeysuckles teased my pallet; shades of childhood, and whispers of days gone by are precious treasures.

"Ms. Mary Mack, Mack, Mack
All dressed in black, black, black
With silver buttons, buttons, buttons

All down her back, back, back"

Olde to the days of childhood...

The Ugly Duckling Phase

Merriam-Webster dictionary defines *an ugly duckling* as a person or thing that seems unpromising but later develops great beauty, talent, or worth.

The budding years for me were a metamorphosis of internal and external changes. The most uncomfortable and shocking experience - undeveloped breasts that ached and crude signals in my pelvic area. I felt like a plain Jane; nothing was striking about me. I was tall for my age, slender, and a late bloomer. No curves, just a straight picket fence. My legs were long, lanky, almost like pipe cleaners; well, that's how I felt. Never a rounding in my school blouse - flat as a pancake! My friends were fortunate. They proudly giggled at the two hills that gracefully redefined their sweaters. My sweater was like a billboard - easy to read. As a teenager, I struggled with my appearance and pondered if the girl in the mirror would ever change. While some of my friends who sported their sweaters with hills gained the boys' attention in our class, I felt alone. The boys would speak to me because they saw me only as a friend, not witty or pretty. I was no one special.

Someone's in my Garden

One day, I boarded the school bus and sat in my usual seat in the mid-section of the bus near the window. My friends sat in front and behind me, so it appeared we had ownership on that side and section of the bus. Truthfully, our voices were distinctly heightened like a bullhorn when we sang or talked. Our bus driver was an elderly gentleman and didn't seem to mind our burst of chatter and laughter. That day, however, felt different, almost sinister – something was wrong. A slightly oversized boy boarded at the next stop; he was a stranger to us. He looked for a seat and saw a space next to me, so he sat down. At first, I didn't notice that he was staring at me and pretended the seat was still empty. He smelt musty, and his clothing was a bit tattered and unclean. With a quick glimpse, I noted his hair was weighted down with oil or perhaps dirty with a slight part to the right side. He smiled back with that dirty, curled lip which made me cringe. He proceeded to press next to me, pushing me against the metal side of the bus and the window. I pushed back and adjusted how I was sitting, which seemed to agitate him, and he pushed even harder - I couldn't move! All at once, he placed his hand under my skirt.

I didn't know what was happening, and I opened my mouth to scream, but there was no sound. I was trapped, terrified of this menacing, looming, musty boy with the curled lip. The sky quickly grayed, and, in my mind, I knew the sun was in protest watching the offense take place – someone was in my garden!

Shocked – Shamed – Scarred and Silenced

Each day, the monster boarded, dressed in another tattered shirt and crinkled pants. His musty, foul smell often sieged the air on the school bus, taking our nostrils captive until he off-boarded. I desperately tried to be first in line so I could get on the bus and sit with someone else, anyone. On those days, I was alone, he sat with me, and the intrusion continued. He probed the sacred core dismantling the place preserved for the one who would love me. The awkward intruder broke my strand without permission, and I scrambled to pick up the pearls. I felt alone on the school bus. I could see my friends and the movement of their lips but could not hear them. I was too afraid to talk about it as he whispered threats in my ear. What did I do? Why did this happen to me? Why did I allow it to happen? WAKE UP! Linda, where are you? I was in shock, disbelief, ashamed, and scared. I felt as dirty as the boy who touched me! I was rudely jolted like a marionette, controlled by the strings of his lust. The trajectory of my life altered forever! I was lost, bewildered and desperately tried to find my way back to the comfort of the sun.

The Island of Misfit Toys

One of the most iconic holiday classics my siblings and I watched every December was Rudolph the Red nosed Reindeer. A particular part of the story that resonates with me is the Island of Misfit Toys. You know the story, there's a kindly lion, King

Moonracer, who is the guardian and welcomes anyone needing lodging. Sadly, many of the occupants are toys that have been discarded because of unique defects. A jack-in-the-box named Charlie, a water gun that shoots jelly, a train with square wheels, a boat that couldn't float, and a doll with some type of mental disorder. I, too, felt like a misfit, damaged and discarded. The intrusions left me paralyzed, and I understood why the doll pulled her hair and talked in riddles. The repeated offenses robbed me, breaking down the doors of my self-worth. As he fumbled to win another goal, I sank into a dark place devoid of sound. There were only silhouettes, images of girls like me, trapped, dancing round and round to warp music in the shrinking place.

The Road Home

It's been years since it happened, and I managed overtime to push back the memories. I moved on with life and tried to forget the face, the smell, and the touch. I busied myself at school and college, traveled, modeled for Barbizon, and accepted catalog work with Sears. My life was getting better, and I felt good about the new chapters, unscathed by past trauma. I fell in love with a gentleman and married him after a time of courtship. Finally, I thought I could escape the haunting memories and fill the bruised space with new dreams and aspirations. Sadly, I was wrong. The time of bliss did not last, and divorce was the best option. The new scars mingled with the old are now a more profound imprint scorching my soul with new lament and pain.

The haunting of yesterday oozed like odorous pus resurfacing, him, his face, his smell, and the touch. Memories forced in the recesses of my mind begin to flood like stagnated waters and I could hear the warp music in the shrinking place. The ancient door flung open wide, and I was triggered anew by the memories and the monster.

I can't go back there!

I won't go back there!

I can't allow the ghost of the past to taunt me any longer!

That was not my fault, but *it is* my fight!

I won't own what I didn't purchase!

It was time to face the monster, find my voice - it was time to take *my life* back!

Like a toddler having a temper tantrum, I stomped my feet and screamed as loud as I could, *I'm gonna tell*!!!!!!

Silk and Satin

In 2015, I was invited to be part of a special pilot group at the House of Ruth. I was nervous but knew this was an open-door opportunity back to wholeness. Listening to the director who shared the outline for the new work, I was confident, God was ordering my steps. I was ready. The group met at a private and safe location. There were a total of seven women, and we were all nervous. The first session, tears and tissues; thank goodness for Puffs with lotion. The group therapy was intentional but gentle as they touched root issues that slowly began to surface. Yes, it was an uncomfortable but necessary step to teach us how to manage triggers while forming the words that gave our stories a new skin.

Over time, we graduated as the first Storytellers for the House of Ruth (Maryland)! Today, we share our stories of suffrage, resilience and triumph for juridical conferences, educational events, hospital training sessions, community agencies, churches and advocates supporting IPV (Intimate Partner Violence) victims during court hearings.

In the biblical account of Tamar, who was beguiled and sexually assaulted by her half-brother, she lost everything! Her royal influence, social status, and dignity. Tamar's intelligence, creativity, and inner peace were all violently disrupted by the lust of her half-brother. The horrid illicit act of sexual trauma changed the trajectory of her future forever. Tamar was culturally erased and pushed back like a lost scroll in history. She was silenced by shame and a resident forever doomed to repeat the waltz of sorrow in the shrinking place.

Today, I honor her story by telling my own in the hope that you will rise from the ashes of your trauma.

You will never heal until the truth is revealed!

The time is now to lose the fetters of your shame!

It's time to turn violation into victory!

I was victimized but NEVER a victim!

If Tamar were here today, she would stand with us! She would be encouraged by our personal testimonies, strengthened by our unity and lifted by the harmony of our voices. She would no longer cower to the cultural conditions of her time but rise as a Phoenix from the ashes of trauma. If she were here today, Tamar would stand with us.

My destiny, *your* destiny, is not predicated on what happened.

So turn your pain into purpose and your shame into success!

Look around; Tamars are standing up everywhere unfettered and releasing their testimonies of resilience and victory!

Come out, Come out wherever you are; Meet a young lady healed from her scars.

I am Tamar, and this is my story!

Mary Mack. (2023, March 11). In *Wikipedia*.
https://en.wikipedia.org/wiki/Mary_Mack

BIOGRAPHY
Dr. Linda Harvey

Apostle Dr. Linda M. Johnson-Harvey is the Visionary, Founder, and Overseer of Fragrance of Faith Ministry, Incorporated. A 501c3 spirit-led organization that has received numerous citations and awards for leadership and the support of marginalized communities. Apostle Dr. Harvey serves as the Apostolic Covering for several ministries, programs, and businesses in Maryland, North Carolina, New Jersey, and Virginia. She celebrates 33 years in ministry, a published book author, psalmist, and mentor. She is a Trauma Facilitator and Coach (Trauma Healing Institute) and a graduate of the first Storyteller Group for House of Ruth Maryland. She is a facilitator/mentor for Maryland Business Roundtable for Education (MBRE) and a Baltimore City Public School Advisory Board member. She's committed to assisting the Chesapeake Bible College and Seminary as an instructor at the Freedom Temple AME Zion Church – satellite center. She continues her educational pursuit and enrichment at Chesapeake Bible College & Seminary and St. Mary's Ecumenical Institute. Dr. Linda Harvey is employed at The Johns Hopkins Hospital in Baltimore and celebrates ten years of professional service.

Dr. Linda Harvey recently received an Honorary Doctorate from the School of the Great Commission (Eastern Shore Satellite Campus), a fully accredited international organization. She was dubbed a "trailblazer" in the community and Christian Education.

Apostle Harvey's mantra, ***"Everyone has the ability to change community."***

She echoes a familiar expression from one of her chosen historical mentors, the late Mary Church Terrell (1st African American woman to earn a degree and was a national activist for civil rights and women's suffrage), ***"Keep everlastingly at it."***

"Let my life be an example of strength and resilience – allow me to be your beckon of hope."

46

Apostle Dr. Linda M. Johnson-Harvey *can be reach*
apostle@lindaharveyministries.com
apostle@fragranceoffaith.com
lmj2010@aol.com
443-562-0093

5

GOD HAS SET ME FREE
Sonya Anissa

"God has smiled on me; He has set me free. God smiled on me; He's been good to me."

I do not recall at what age I learned that song, but I remember singing it in church, and I have heard it repeatedly in my mind for years. Not until a particular moment did, I really understand what that song meant. As a matter of fact, I didn't feel like God was smiling on me for most of my life. I went through the motions like I had been taught; singing, praying, volunteering at church, and even raising my children in the church. Just to be clear, it was not that I did not believe in God or that I did not have faith. It was that I was not worthy of His smile. I had seen what God would do and could do for others, but I had such low self-esteem that I never put myself in the category of those who could receive His smile.

My journey to freedom in Jesus Christ has been filled with just about every emotion a person could possibly experience. It all began when I was just seven or eight years old. I was an unassuming and trusting child at that time, just like Tamar. I had no reason to believe that I would be in harm's way in the presence of family members. That, unfortunately, was not the case. My innocence was violated repeatedly throughout my childhood. The words of the community of faith I was a part of at that time led me to believe that I was to follow the instructions without question. I was so young that I did not know I was supposed to tell of the horrific ordeal I was experiencing. As time passed, I realized that being sexually violated was not something to keep secret. I was too ashamed to tell anyone for fear of being looked at with disgust. I had been brainwashed to believe that nobody would believe me and that I would be my family's downfall if I ever told my truth. I felt like I wore the mark of an unworthy sinner. I was silenced before I even knew I had a voice. That silence I was coerced into living with at such a young age began a lifetime of silence and hiding. I lived life under the radar in practically every way.

I rarely did anything that would draw attention to me. The few things that I did do, amongst others, were so that I could blend into the scene. Even with the attempts to go unnoticed, I was still raped at the age of 13 by a family member. I became pregnant as a result of that act and, subsequently, had a termination procedure. I was ill and disgusted in every fiber of my being for the person who violated me and for the decision I made at age 14. I believed that my life was meant to be one of turmoil. The only worth I seemingly had was the most intimate part of me, and that had now been violated to the point of no return, in my opinion. I struggled to see myself as someone that could be of value to others. I devalued myself before I even realized that I was doing it. I allowed family members, peers, and almost everyone to walk over me. I would take whatever was dished out because I believed I deserved it. I wore my shame like a protective shield. It guarded me from being hurt no matter how I was treated because there was nothing another person could do to hurt me that I had not already endured.

My feeling of worthlessness weighed me down, but I was not about to let anyone see that. I remained in my silence, but nobody knew I was being silenced. Thinking about it now, I believed I was seen as the quiet, shy, plain girl who was just there. I had the seemingly ordinary life that I should have lived. I was able to mask almost everything that I disliked about myself. I do think my low self-esteem was prominent, though. I tried to hide that too, but I had an issue with looking in the mirror or anything that reflected my likeness and seeing a vision of beauty. I have thought countless times about how my life might have been different had I spoken up for myself. I am not just thinking of the molestation or the rape but the other instances where others mistreated, devalued, or disrespected me. During friendships, dating, my first marriage, and work-related incidents, I had trained myself to keep my mouth shut, my head down, and my opinions to myself because I felt like I was not worth hearing or seeing. In my efforts to go unnoticed, I developed a stubbornness rivaling some of them. I wore my mask so well that I didn't even know who I was when I took it off. Then a divine encounter changed my perspective.

During a worship service call to the altar, I felt the Holy Spirit speak to me and tell me to release the issues that had plagued me for so long. I began to cry and speak to the things I had been carrying. I cast them at the feet of my Savior, and He released me from the bondage of guilt, shame, regret, fear, disgust, low self-esteem, and fear of rejection. The more I called out, the more He released me. There had been such a cloud over my life in my mind that I had been trying to disappear so no one would see me. This call to the altar was where I yielded to the Spirit and allowed Him to remove all those things and the mask that had become my identity to the world. My Tamar experience had stolen my identity, and I had been living a false existence. I intended to take back everything I had been robbed of, but that was a different experience than I had anticipated.

In this newfound light and life, I became more vocal in all areas of my life. It was a challenge and a process, but slowly I began to emerge. I developed as cautiously as I could because I was still that withdrawn little girl on the inside. It was as if I was battling myself. Because this was new for me, I sought help through counseling. I did my homework- journaling, letter-writing, etc.- and it helped, but my most crucial effort toward healing had yet to come. I could function in all my life aspects, and my relationship with God was continuously strengthened. That experience had shaken me up all those years ago, but as I stated earlier, I had a very robust stubbornness about myself. That did not disappear. I adamantly went back and forth about my self-worth and self-esteem, and it took a very long time for me to get to the point where I was okay with just being "me.". I allowed myself to look through the lens of my Savior. The saying I remember when I have moments of doubt is, "God don't create no junk!" The struggle is real, but my God is more real than any thought I can create. I was created in His image, and there is nothing about me that He has not already endured on my behalf. There was still a problem, though. I had not forgiven my violator or myself.

There had been no legal involvement, public ridicule, or nothing for the violator, and I did not want vindication that way. It had been over twenty years, and I was exhausted from carrying the emotional baggage related to the violation. I had packed those emotions down until they were physically a part of me. This was yet another way I had learned to mask how I felt. Medical issues that could be corrected with a bit of discipline came to the surface. At a doctor's appointment, I heard a voice say, "You have work to do, and it is not optional." I had a similar encounter when I gave the Lord my "Yes," and knew then that things were about to change. I went home and sat with my Bible in my hands, clutched against my chest. I prayed to God and asked for the power to forgive the violator in my heart and head. I then prayed for the strength to forgive myself. I had held myself hostage to that which God had never given to me. My healing was not through the punishment of my violator but through God's grace and mercy toward me. I read several scriptures again and again. At first, I was offended because I kept relating them back to the violator, but as I read Ecclesiastes 3:1-15 KJV and 2 Corinthians 5:16a, 22-23 KJV, I saw myself. If I was created in His image, then even my Tamar experience could not keep me from being what He designed me to be. God is in control, and what He has for me was created for me.

The things I have experienced do not negate that destiny, and I finally accepted that. I am Tamar, but He is God, El Shaddai (Lord God Almighty), Jehovah-Raah (He is my Shepherd), Jehovah Rapha (He Heals), Jehovah Shammah (He is There), Jehovah Jireh (My Provider), and that is all I need.

I am Tamar, and this is my story!

God has smiled on me. Retrieved May 13, 2023, from Retrhttps://www.lyricsondemand.com/r/revjamesclevelandlyrics/godhassmiledonmelyrics.html

BIOGRAPHY
Sonya Anissa

Sonya Anissa is one of the hosts of Mind Matters, a show dedicated to eradicating mental health stigma, streaming on the Black House Collaborations Network (BHC). She founded M.I.D.A.A.S Foundation, a ministry that provides inspiration, encouragement, and empowerment through Mentoring, Informing Diligently, and Assisting, Advocating for, and Supporting Individuals and families who live or are associated with developmental and mental health disabilities. Sonya earned her Master of Arts in Clinical Mental Health Counseling from South University and her Bachelor of Science in Interdisciplinary Studies from Norfolk State University. Sonya Anissa is a Certified Life Coach focusing on Special Needs Life Quality, Resilience, and Empowerment. She is also a Certified Family Peer Support Specialist and a Certified Autism Spectrum Disorder Clinical Specialist. Sonya is a 30+ year veteran of the developmental services and behavioral health population. In addition to being a faith-filled, licensed minister, Sonya is an active Zeta Phi Beta Sorority, Incorporated member. The accomplishment of which Sonya Anissa is most proud is that of being the mother of her two adult children and a grandmother.

Facebook- Sonya Anissa

Instagram- msniecy9270

Twitter @SonyaAnissa1727

YouTube @sanissaspeaks

Email sonya_anissa@outlook.com

midaasfoundation@gmail.com

6

FROM SILENCED TO SILENCER
Maia Johnson

Silence is the absence of noise, but it can be so profound that it seems deafening. Silence can leave someone confused, but it can also be the answer someone needs. Silence can be to someone's detriment or their benefit. For me, silence has felt like a dark, impenetrable, unchanging, and suffocating prison cell. I suffered in silence for years, and it felt like I was locked inside a cell *with* a key but blind to its presence. It was not until I allowed God to show me the key to the cell of silence that freedom became my reality.

There were experiences in my life that gradually chipped away at my voice and silenced me in ways that only trauma can. I witnessed domestic violence and physical altercations between family members and neighbors at a very young age and throughout my childhood. I heard numerous arguments filled with obscenities and threats. I can remember wanting to say something in protest, but I was so young and did not have the language to do so. I wanted to help the one being hurt, but I was powerless. I felt so saddened for the women I saw getting beaten and the men I witnessed fighting each other. I don't think I can ever forget the anger and rage on the faces of the abusers, coupled with the fear of the ones being hit or abused. It always scared me to see them like that. My takeaway was that becoming angry would lead to fighting and pain.

As I grew up, I never allowed myself to appropriately deal with feelings of anger, hurt, or disappointment as I did not want to get angry. I always did my best to stay out of the way of aggressive personalities and out of any trouble that could lead to violence. I never wanted to be the perpetrator or the victim. This may seem like a good decision, but it drastically affected my personality. I became a people-pleaser, constantly compromising on what was best for me in relationships and friendships. If I could keep everyone happy, I would not anger anyone or myself and ultimately not be threatened by physical violence. There were so many times I should have stood up for myself, but time and time again, the trauma of witnessing violence silenced me.

I remember the night it happened. It was a sleepover. We played and had fun. When it was time for bed, we settled down for the night. What happened next would shake me to my core for years and come back to me in fuzzy images. She turned over and lay on top of me. Face pressed so close to mine. I was shocked and confused. I tried to speak, but my voice felt trapped in my throat. The fear and shock gripped me. I lived with the regret of not screaming, running, or telling someone. There would be other instances of being taken advantage of, and again, I said nothing. These experiences caused me to have unhealthy boundaries and toxic relationships. I allowed myself to remain in relationships where I was verbally and mentally abused. I was gaslit and made to believe that I was too sensitive and did not hear and see what I knew I had. This turned into me not trusting myself to see circumstances clearly and accurately. I constantly second-guessed myself and doubted my decision-making.

Throughout my life, I struggled with low self-esteem and sought validation of my worth in the attention I received from men.

I never thought about what was best for me and tried to be perfect for everyone else. I thought the best of everyone even when they showed they did not deserve it. Constant compromise and choosing others instead of choosing what was best for me was how I operated in relationships and friendships. I allowed myself to be mistreated in friendships and allowed people to use me. I knew they were envious and sought to sabotage me, but I explained it away, not to address it. It was unclear to me what should and should not be allowed in relationships and friendships because boundaries that should not have been crossed were, and it left me with a skewed view. I constantly gave people chances to prove their intentions toward me wrong, but things did not change. I did not know how to leave when being emotionally and mentally abused. I did not realize that I deserved better. This led to extreme insecurity and trust issues. I stayed when I should have left and said nothing when I should have spoken—the trauma of being taken advantage of silenced me.

Rejection is a pain that is not easily forgotten. When that rejection comes from a place that you have no control over or ability to change, it can be even more piercing. I was bullied and rejected because of the color of my skin. "High yellow," "house slave," and "redbone" were some of the names I was called. I was told I thought I was "all that because I was light-skinned with long hair." All the while, I struggled with low self-esteem and low self-worth. I was picked on for not being "black enough." Growing up, I loved it when the summer months rolled around so I could get a tan from the sun because then I would not be taunted for my fair skin. I constantly downplayed any hints of beauty because I feared it would make others uncomfortable. I felt ashamed to embrace my skin, my looks, and who I was because it could make others envious and angry. I did not pursue friendships and kept to myself for fear of being rejected for simply being who and how God made me.

Another instance of trauma that occurred in my life was regarding my writing. I believe that writing is a gift God gave me, and I enjoyed writing stories as a preteen. I think I liked the fact that it was a way for me to express myself without speaking. I wrote a story once and wanted my English teacher, who I greatly respected, to read it. The story was about a child who was being abused. I saw a made for tv movie about a similar storyline, and it inspired me. I wanted to write a story about how a child overcame the pain. When I was done, I brought the story to school for my teacher to read. She became quiet as she went through it and asked me if I was being abused. I was not and told her no. She then said something that I would never forget. She said I should not write such stories because people would not want to read them. I felt rejected and crushed and would not write for enjoyment for the next 20 years. I was ashamed and embarrassed. While I understand the subject matter was unorthodox, it was a story of overcoming. Nothing could have prepared me for what happened in the coming days. My English teacher came to school one-day wearing sunglasses. She exited the classroom after homeroom started, and the sunglasses were gone when she returned. With the glasses removed, the black eye she had was revealed. I was left so confused. The trauma of her rejection silenced me.

For many years, I had been reluctant to deal with the pain of the trauma. My coping mechanism was to avoid it or run. I would run away from or avoid, in my mind, every circumstance that caused me pain. I also fell into the comparison trap. The devil would speak lies like, "What are you upset about? What you went through was not that bad." "What do you need counseling for? Some people have been through worse than you." The one that silenced me each time was, "People are going to laugh at you because you could have stopped it, but you didn't." When memories of the trauma surfaced, I would compare them to other people's trauma. If their trauma seemed worse than mine, I explained away that my experiences could not possibly be defined as traumatic. The devil would play mind games and gaslight me into doubting myself to prevent me from dealing with the pain and issues.

In 2015, I could no longer run, and I learned that scars are not always visible because the emotional scars that I had, surfaced undeniably. I was experiencing panic attacks, anxiety, nightmares, and emotional and physical pain when the memories came back to me in haunting images. My back was against the wall, and I either had to allow God to expose and heal the pain or remain bound by the pain. It was so freeing for me when I verbally acknowledged to God those traumatic experiences from childhood to adulthood (Psalms 118:5 KJV). The residue of the trauma had affected every facet of my life, motherhood, marriage, and relationships. I had to partner with God and do the work to experience healing.

This process began with forgiveness. I had to forgive those who had hurt, used, and taken advantage of me (Matthew 6:14 KJV). I had to forgive those that caused me to feel worthless so that they could feel better about themselves. Forgiving myself was most important for me in my healing process (Ephesians 4:32 KJV and Romans 8:1 KJV). For so long, I told myself, had I just made different decisions, had I screamed or yelled, or had I told someone, none of what I had experienced would have ever happened. I hated myself for a long time for being "weak" and silenced in situations when I should have spoken. Far too many times, I allowed myself to remain silent, and I was ashamed and despised myself for it. As I embarked on the healing process, God showed me it was not my fault. Pain that others inflicted on me was not requested or warranted, so no, it was never my fault. Even my response to the trauma was nothing to be ashamed of. I did not have the tools to communicate or deal with the trauma appropriately. I forgave myself for not honoring myself because, simply put, I did not know how to.

The Lord took me through a season where, day in and day out, He exposed the lies I believed for so long. He took me back and showed me how the devil had silenced me. He showed me the sin I needed deliverance from because of doors that had been opened by my forefathers and myself. He showed me the generational sins I operated in that I had to denounce and renounce. God showed me how to repent for my sins, forgive myself, and release false burdens. He showed me how to forgive others (Ephesians 4:32 KJV). Did confronting the memories hurt? Yes, it did, but no more than it did when I was being hurt. The process to address it was necessary. God is intentional about all He does and will not put more on you than you can handle (Matthew 11:28-30 KJV). He can be trusted in the healing process.

I attended counseling and received personalized ministry to deal with the pain of the trauma from bullying, molestation, people-pleasing, and unhealthy boundaries. On this journey, I would become triggered by things I saw and heard. It could be a song, the tone of someone's voice, or even a tv show or scene in a movie. The triggers would sometimes take me right back to that emotionally saddened state. It took a lot of prayers, praise, worship, confessing the word of God, and even tears to get past the past. I stand today as a witness to the healing power of Jesus Christ (Psalms 147:3). Over time, the triggers were not as painful. I could identify beforehand those things that could potentially pull me backward in my healing journey. Sometimes, I would become very anxious at the thought of the enemy sending fiery darts (Ephesians 6:16 KJV). Gradually, I began to welcome the triggers. I used them as a gauge of how much I had progressed in addressing those things that attempted to threaten me on my path to healing. God took those things that had power over my life and rendered them powerless (Ephesians 1:19-21 KJV). I am not perfect at dealing with triggers, but I am far from where I used to be, and I thank God for it. I know that the triggers will come, but I remind myself of the finished work of Jesus on the Cross and that, indeed, by His stripes, I am healed (Isaiah 53:5 KJV).

In the healing process, I have often wondered how I would get through the pain. I did not understand how God could turn terrible into something great (Genesis 50:20 KJV). I want to encourage you that the pain will not be wasted. God will use it to do extraordinary things in you and through you once you give it to

Him and allow Him to heal you. He silenced the devil's lies and spoke the truth to my heart and mind. He silenced the voice of the devil and voiced His love and acceptance. The devil used trauma to silence my voice, and even when I used writing as a means "to speak," he also attempted to take that. However, I have recaptured my voice and am using it to help others.

Glory be to God that I stand today, no longer silenced. I have gone from *silenced to the silencer*. A silencer is a part that is placed on a firearm to reduce the noise of the gunshot. I am using my voice to silence the lies and speak the truth. The Lord has positioned me to write to encourage those silenced to receive healing and reclaim their voice. I am no longer bound and am taking my position, sounding my voice and shouting, "Whom the Son makes free is free indeed" (John 8:32 KJV). I am using my voice to do what the enemy said I should not and could not do, writing to encourage others to heal from the pain. I want to encourage others to confront the trauma and acknowledge that no weapon formed against you prospered (Isaiah. 54:17 KJV). I write to encourage you that you, too, can be free of the heartache as you allow the Father to heal you (Psalms 147:3 KJV). God has done it for me; He can and will do it for you. A generation needs our voices to help them overcome the trauma. Will you partner with God to be healed and be used by Him to be a conduit of healing and deliverance for others? It is time for the silenced to become silencers!

I am Tamar, and this is my story!

BIOGRAPHY
Maia Johnson

Maia Johnson is a woman of God, wife, mother, intercessor, and author. She holds a Bachelor of Arts in Communicative Sciences and Disorders from Hampton University and a Master of Science in Speech-Language Pathology from Old Dominion University. Mrs. Johnson has worked as a speech-language pathologist; however, her most rewarding work was as a stay-at-home Mom, using her professional talents to homeschool her children. She has served as a minister, teacher, intercessor, and women's ministry leader.

Maia is an educator who enjoys the privilege of instructing students. She is a member of Hampton Roads Women for Education, Inc. This non-profit organization supports the academic endeavors of elementary, middle, high school, and college students. She is an avid writer and, in January 2023, self-published her first book on Amazon, *Devotions for the Heart*, a collection of devotions for those who seek to live a life with a heart that personifies God's heart. Maia is passionate about seeing the brokenhearted healed and the bound set free. Maia lives in Chesapeake, Virginia, with her husband, Craig, and their four children.

Facebook: Maia Johnson
Instagram: maiaj4everhis_jc.

7

HEALED TO BE MADE WHOLE
Natasha Jones

I sat on the bed, surrounded by my Bible, journal, pen, and the knowledge that I must forgive. I had been having this recurring dream in which I was vomiting nonstop. Every time I tried to speak, I would vomit again. And it wasn't what you would imagine. Instead, it was a bitter, putrid substance with a taste that remained even after I woke up. No matter how much I tried, I could not get rid of that taste. I couldn't wash it away. I couldn't pray it away. I couldn't wish it away. I soon came to learn I had to forgive it away.

And so I began my journey of forgiveness with my then-marriage. It was the current source of my greatest pain. I was full of hurt, brokenness, and anger. I could not believe what was happening. None of it made sense in light of what God promised us. All the prophetic declarations that had been spoken over us.

There was no way this was what had become of the romance I once shared with my first love. Never in my wildest dream did I imagine he would be out of the house and me with our two little babies alone and heartbroken. Depressed.

As I sat in that spot in the middle of the bed, emotionally in the depths of depression, unable to get up and complete simple tasks like taking my teenager to school, God showed me the enemy's plan to destroy me. He showed me a dry and desolate place, the ground like hardened dust, cracked from the dryness. It was worse than a desert land with no water or greenery around, and there I sat, in the middle of it.

Alone.

Broken.

That vision from the Lord gave me just enough energy to rise up and fight. I was determined not to let the devil win. Despite the pain I'd endured from childhood, the betrayal and heartbreak I'd experienced in my marriage, I had to persevere. And as I sat on that bed with my baby sleeping beside me, I cried out to God to show me! "Lord, what is the root of this? Why does it hurt so badly? What am I supposed to do? How do you want me to forgive after all of this?" And He took me back to childhood. God showed me the pain I was carrying was there all along. Only the current situation in my marriage brought it to the surface. My marriage that represented safety was tattered, and that gave way to every memory of every time I did not feel safe to arise.

I think the first memory that came up was me crying to my mother, asking her why she'd allowed bad things to happen to me. I cried to her, shaking, "Why did you allow them to hurt me like that?!" Even though the actual conversation with her had occurred probably 15 years or more prior, I could still hear her voice, feel her touch, and remember exactly what she said. She must have thought her words were comforting, but they brought nothing but additional pain to me. "It's gonna be alright." But it wasn't alright. It wasn't alright when I cried to her, and it wasn't alright as these and other memories arose. Memories of the molestations from my childhood. Memories of the police coming and taking the report. I still had the vivid imagery of where I was standing in my childhood home, what I was wearing, and the terror running through me as the police officer beckoned me to sit on his lap and tell him what happened. I remember freezing, afraid to move. It was as if I was trying to disappear.

Sometime after that, my dad stopped by to visit. We were on the back porch, and he was sitting down. I was standing, and he motioned for me to sit on his knee. My father was always this way with me. Very gentle, very loving, and adoring. But that day, when he requested, I sat on his knee, I froze. I was afraid. I felt the same fear and anxiety I felt the night the police officer asked me to sit on his knee and tell him what happened. My dad noticed something was wrong, and he asked what it was. I shrugged as if to say I didn't know, and I never told him. I was afraid of what would happen if I told him. While my dad was always very gentle with me, he was a wild man in the streets. It was all too complicated in my head. There was no best-case scenario, and I didn't want to be the cause of the families feuding in the neighborhood. My dad kind of resigned himself to me backing away with an okay and didn't push me to sit on his knee again. If I had known my father would be murdered a few years later, I would have excitedly sat on his knee and hugged him as tightly and long as I could.

I later learned I had no control over that freezing response, that my brain chose for me what was safest and what would keep me alive in that situation. This freezing response would come up so many times over the years that followed. When I faced an unsafe situation or a situation, I perceived to be unsafe, I would freeze. There were other things too. I became hypervigilant, always on the alert for any situation that seemed suspicious. I created tall, strong, super-fortified walls all around me. I erected boundaries to keep others out because I'd learned through those adverse childhood experiences that allowing people to be close was not safe.

I maintained these boundaries extremely well. I kept everyone at a distance. But that changed in 7th grade when I met my first love. He was safe to me. He seemed to love me for me, which made me realize how I viewed all other relationships as transactional. My past relations prior to meeting him were based on me meeting a need or an expectation for someone else in exchange for love or acceptance. These patterns have been present for as long as I can remember.

And because my boundaries were so sacred to me, I would do anything to protect them, even if it involved fighting. From elementary to high school, I developed a reputation for throwing hands. Some people labeled me as mean. Some adults knew there had to be something going on. I was a walking paradox, extremely intelligent and extremely ready to fight. It was another part of my system choosing how to protect me, and then, it became part of my identity. I distinctly remember a principal once telling my mother how the school staff and administrators had tried everything to get me off a girl during a fight, and grown men could not stop me. My mother nodded with understanding, saying, "That's my daughter." She was familiar with it; I fought at home and in the neighborhood too. I was never going to let someone have the upper hand with me again. I took my protection seriously, and I fought to keep people away.

So, in my room, in the middle of my bed, God began to deal with me. First, He assured my safety. He chose the best time, the right place, and certainly the most appropriate situation. He got me alone, and He processed me. Some moments felt easy, like, "I got this." Other moments were ugly. They were knocked down, dragged out ugly. I wanted answers. I wanted to know why. I wanted revenge. I wanted God to do stuff to the people that hurt me. I experienced every emotion imaginable. And through God's grace, I made it through the process. God began to replace the stone in my heart with flesh. He would bring up the memory, and we dealt with it together until I could forgive. That process took me from a private decision of forgiveness to publicly confronting one of the abusers with forgiveness. This is what happened.

We were at a family gathering, and the individual was about to step out. I invited myself to join him. The conversation commenced with general pleasantries, and outwardly, all was well. But on the inside, my heart was pounding. I was in fight mode. My nervous system was perceiving threats. I had already played it out in my mind that they would deny they had sexually abused me or act like I was crazy or something. So, I was ready to fight... but I had to focus on the most important fight, which was the fight for my freedom, freedom that could only come through forgiveness.

I began to express to the individual that what they had done to me when I was a child was very hurtful and that it was still emotionally hard at various times throughout my life. I didn't go into a lot of detail because I needed to stick to the plan to serve notice that I forgave them. So, I told them despite the pain and all that happened, I was bringing it up because I wanted them to know I forgave them. I said it, "I forgive you."

With those simple words, I released all the rights I held to anger, hurt, payback, revenge, or ill intent. I released the years of emotional drain and dread I'd lived. And I was done.

Then, the most unpredictable thing happened.

The person apologized. Sincerely apologize. They said they were sorry and didn't know I had been carrying that with me all those years. If they could take it back, they would.

And suddenly, I felt soft without being fully aware of how tense I was. Gone was the hardness of anger, bitterness, unforgiveness, and tension. All of my crutches and everything I used to shield me from hurt. I never expected it to be so freeing.

But God did.

He knew all along what was on the other side of forgiveness for me. He knew I was too precious to Him to be unhealed. He knew what it would take to make me whole.

But deeper than that, God knew the purpose behind the pain I lived. You see, I forgave many years before I ever had therapy. It wasn't that I hadn't tried to get therapy; I just couldn't find the right therapist for me. And again, God knew what was on the other side of that process. As I searched, searched, and did not find, I realized I had in me what I was seeking. And that if I was seeking it, surely others like me were also seeking it. And it informed my decision to become what I needed, a Black female Christian therapist. It propelled me in the direction of the destiny God had preordained for my life as a healer.

During that healing process, I spent many more nights with God in the middle of my bed. Just me and Him. And the issues that caused the brokenness. I'm blessed to say I've never had to forgive for that same abuse again. I see that person now and feel nothing toward them. Through God-led forgiveness, I was made whole in that area of my life, and I am grateful never to have another dream of bitter vomit again.

The adults I needed to protect me did not, but GOD DID. He healed me to make me whole.

I am Tamar, and this is my story!

BIOGRAPHY
Natasha Jones

With the death of a doting father and becoming a mom at 14, there is no doubt the work she does is the answer to a Calling. Dr. Natasha Jones is the go-to therapist for women seeking to heal from past traumas and resolve the blocks that keep them stuck. She is a no holds barred Believer who is indignant about suffering in the children of God.

In addition to her career as a Professional Consultant & Coach, Natasha is the proprietor of Whole Village Counseling, an outpatient counseling and mental wellness center in Hampton Roads. She is also the founder of Whole Village Healing Services, Inc., a 501(c)(3) non-profit organization with a mission of improving the health & wellness of minorities living in/experiencing poverty in the Hampton Roads Region through education, access, and support.

Dr. Jones holds a Master's degree in Counselor Education and a Ph.D. in Clinical Health Psychology from Virginia State University. She enjoys spending time with her family, reading a good book, and doing nothing at all. Natasha is also the author of Until My Next Session, a Guided Journal For Women In Therapy, and it is available on Amazon.

Dr. Natasha Jones can be reached at
thesoulcaretherapist@gmail.com
www.facebook.com/natashajoybellsjones
www.instagram.com/natashaljones

8

BREAK A LEG
Mia Overton-Smith

Silence.

Silence is the absence of noise, but it can be so profound that it seems deafening. Silence can leave someone confused, but it can also be the answer someone needs. Silence can be to someone's detriment or their benefit. For me, silence has felt like a dark, impenetrable, unchanging, and suffocating prison cell. I suffered in silence for years, and it felt like I was locked inside a cell *with* a key but blind to its presence. It was not until I allowed God to show me the key to the cell of silence that freedom became my reality.

There were experiences in my life that gradually chipped away at my voice and silenced me in ways that only trauma can. I witnessed domestic violence and physical altercations between family members and neighbors at a very young age and throughout my childhood. I heard numerous arguments filled with obscenities and threats. I can remember wanting to say something in protest, but I was so young and did not have the language to do so. I wanted to help the one being hurt, but I was powerless. I felt so saddened for the women I saw getting beaten and the men I witnessed fighting each other. I don't think I can ever forget the anger and rage on the faces of the abusers, coupled with the fear of the ones being hit or abused. It always scared me to see them like that. My takeaway was that becoming angry would lead to fighting and pain.

As I grew up, I never allowed myself to appropriately deal with feelings of anger, hurt, or disappointment as I did not want to get angry. I always did my best to stay out of the way of aggressive personalities and out of any trouble that could lead to violence. I never wanted to be the perpetrator or the victim. This may seem like a good decision, but it drastically affected my personality. I became a people-pleaser, constantly compromising on what was best for me in relationships and friendships. If I could keep everyone happy, I would not anger anyone or myself and ultimately not be threatened by physical violence. There were so many times I should have stood up for myself, but time and time again, the trauma of witnessing violence silenced me.

I remember the night it happened. It was a sleepover. We played and had fun. When it was time for bed, we settled down for the night. What happened next would shake me to my core for years and come back to me in fuzzy images. She turned over and lay on top of me. Face pressed so close to mine. I was shocked and confused. I tried to speak, but my voice felt trapped in my throat. The fear and shock gripped me. I lived with the regret of not screaming, running, or telling someone. There would be other instances of being taken advantage of, and again, I said nothing. These experiences caused me to have unhealthy boundaries and toxic relationships. I allowed myself to remain in relationships where I was verbally and mentally abused. I was gaslit and made to believe that I was too sensitive and did not hear and see what I knew I had. This turned into me not trusting myself to see circumstances clearly and accurately. I constantly second-guessed myself and doubted my decision-making.

Throughout my life, I struggled with low self-esteem and sought validation of my worth in the attention I received from men. I never thought about what was best for me and tried to be perfect for everyone else. I thought the best of everyone even when they showed they did not deserve it. Constant compromise and choosing others instead of choosing what was best for me was how I operated in relationships and friendships. I allowed myself to be mistreated in friendships and allowed people to use me. I knew they were envious and sought to sabotage me, but I explained it away, not to address it. It was unclear to me what should and should not be allowed in relationships and friendships because boundaries that should not have been crossed were, and it left me with a skewed view. I constantly gave people chances to prove their intentions toward me wrong, but things did not change. I did not know how to leave when being emotionally and mentally abused. I did not realize that I deserved better. This led to extreme insecurity and trust issues. I stayed when I should have left and said nothing when I should have spoken. The trauma of being taken advantage of silencing me.

Rejection is a pain that is not easily forgotten. When that

rejection comes from a place that you have no control over or ability to change, it can be even more piercing. I was bullied and rejected because of the color of my skin. "High yellow," "house slave," and "redbone" were some of the names I was called. I was told I thought I was "all that because I was light-skinned with long hair." All the while, I struggled with low self-esteem and low self-worth. I was picked on for not being "black enough." Growing up, I loved it when the summer months rolled around so I could get a tan from the sun because then I would not be taunted for my fair skin. I constantly downplayed any hints of beauty because I feared it would make others uncomfortable. I felt ashamed to embrace my skin, my looks, and who I was because it could make others envious and angry. I did not pursue friendships and kept to myself for fear of being rejected for simply being who and how God made me.

Another instance of trauma that occurred in my life was regarding my writing. I believe that writing is a gift God gave me, and I enjoyed writing stories as a preteen. I think I liked the fact that it was a way for me to express myself without speaking. I wrote a story once and wanted my English teacher, who I greatly respected, to read it. The story was about a child who was being abused. I saw a made for tv movie about a similar storyline, and it inspired me. I wanted to write a story about how a child overcame the pain. When I was done, I brought the story to school for my teacher to read. She became quiet as she went through it and asked me if I was being abused. I was not and told her no. She then said something that I would never forget. She said I should not write such stories because people would not want to read them. I felt rejected and crushed and would not write for enjoyment for the next 20 years. I was ashamed and embarrassed. While I understand the subject matter was unorthodox, it was a story of overcoming. Nothing could have prepared me for what happened in the coming days. My English teacher came to school one-day wearing sunglasses. She exited the classroom after homeroom started, and the sunglasses were gone when she returned. With the glasses removed, the black eye she had was revealed. I was left so confused. The trauma of her rejection silenced me.

For many years, I had been reluctant to deal with the pain of the trauma. My coping mechanism was to avoid it or run. I run away from or avoid, in my mind, every circumstance that caused me pain. I also fell into the comparison trap. The devil would speak lies like, "What are you upset about? What you went through was not that bad." "What do you need counseling for? Some people have been through worse than you." The one that silenced me each time was, "People are going to laugh at you because you could have stopped it, but you didn't." When the traumatic memories surfaced, I would compare them to other people's trauma. If their trauma seemed worse than mine, I explained away that my experiences could not possibly be defined as traumatic. The devil would play mind games and gaslight me into doubting myself to prevent me from dealing with the pain and issues.

In 2015, I could no longer run, and I learned that scars are not always visible because the emotional scars that I had, surfaced undeniably. I was experiencing panic attacks, anxiety, nightmares, and emotional and physical pain when the trauma memories came back to me in haunting images. My back was against the wall, and I either had to allow God to expose and heal the pain or remain bound by the pain. It was so freeing for me when I verbally acknowledged to God those traumatic experiences from childhood to adulthood (Psalms 118:5 KJV). The residue of the trauma had affected every facet of my life, motherhood, marriage, and relationships. I had to partner with God and do the work to experience healing.

This process began with forgiveness. I had to forgive those who had hurt, used, and taken advantage of me (Matthew 6:14 KJV). I had to forgive those that caused me to feel worthless so that they could feel better about themselves. Forgiving myself was most important for me in my healing process (Ephesians 4:32 KJV and Romans 8:1 KJV). For so long, I told myself, had I just made different decisions, had I screamed or yelled, or had I told someone, none of what I had experienced would have ever happened. I hated myself for a long time for being "weak" and silenced in situations when I should have spoken. Far too many times, I allowed myself to remain silent, and I was ashamed and despised myself for it. As I embarked on the healing process, God showed me it was not my fault. Pain that others inflicted on me was not requested or warranted, so no, it was never my fault. Even my response to the trauma was nothing to be ashamed of. I did not have the tools to communicate or deal with the trauma appropriately. I forgave myself for not honoring myself because, simply put, I did not know how to.

The Lord took me through a season where, day in and day out, He exposed the lies I believed for so long. He took me back and showed me how the devil had silenced me. He showed me the sin I needed deliverance from because of doors that had been opened by my forefathers and myself. He showed me the generational sins I operated in that had to be denounced, renounced, and repented. God showed me how to forgive myself and release false burdens. He showed me how to forgive others (Ephesians 4:32 KJV). Did confronting the memories hurt? Yes, it did, but no more than it did when I was being hurt. The process to address it was necessary. God is intentional about all He does and will not put more on you than you can handle (Matthew 11:28-30 KJV). He can be trusted in the healing process.

I attended counseling and received personalized ministry to deal with the pain of the trauma from bullying, molestation, people-pleasing, and unhealthy boundaries. On this journey, I would become triggered by things I saw and heard. It could be a song, the tone of someone's voice, or even a tv show or scene in a movie. The triggers would sometimes take me right back to that emotionally saddened state. It took a lot of prayers, praise, worship, confessing the word of God, and even tears to get past the past. I stand today as a witness to the healing power of Jesus Christ (Psalms 147:3). Over time, the triggers were not as painful. I could identify beforehand those things that could potentially pull me backward in my healing journey. Sometimes, I would become very anxious at the thought of the enemy sending fiery darts (Ephesians 6:16 KJV). Gradually, I began to welcome the triggers. I used them as a gauge of how much I had progressed in addressing those things that attempted to threaten me on my path to healing. God took those things that had power over my life and rendered them powerless (Ephesians 1:19-21 KJV). I am not perfect at dealing with triggers, but I am far from where I used to be, and I thank God for it. I know that the triggers will come, but I remind myself of the finished work of Jesus on the Cross and that, indeed, by His stripes, I am healed (Isaiah 53:5 KJV).

In the healing process, I have often wondered how I would get through the pain. I did not understand how God could turn terrible into something great (Genesis 50:20 KJV). I want to encourage you that the pain will not be wasted. God will use it to do extraordinary things in you and through you once you give it to Him and allow Him to heal you. He silenced the devil's lies and spoke the truth to my heart and mind. He silenced the voice of the devil and voiced His love and acceptance. The devil used trauma to silence my voice, and even when I used writing as a means "to speak," he also attempted to take that. However, I have recaptured my voice and am using it to help others.

Glory be to God that I stand today, no longer silenced. I have gone from *silenced to the silencer*. A silencer is a part that is placed on a firearm to reduce the noise of the gunshot. I am using my voice to silence the lies and speak the truth. The Lord has positioned me to write to encourage those silenced to receive healing and reclaim their voice. I am no longer bound and am taking my position, sounding my voice and shouting, "Whom the Son makes free is free indeed" (John 8:32 KJV). I am using my voice to do what the enemy said I should not and could not do, writing to encourage others to heal from the pain. I want to encourage others to confront the trauma and acknowledge that no weapon formed against you prospered (Isaiah. 54:17 KJV). I write to encourage you that you, too, can be free of the heartache as you allow the Father to heal you (Psalms 147:3 KJV). God has done it for me; He can and will do it for you. A generation needs our voices to help them overcome the trauma. Will you partner with God to be healed and be used by Him to be a conduit of healing and deliverance for others? It is time for the silenced to become silencers!

I am Tamar, and this is my story!

BIOGRAPHY
Mia Overton-Smith

Mia Deneen Smith is a native of Virginia Beach, Virginia. She is a devoted wife and mother of three beautiful children. She holds a Bachelor's degree in Music and a Master of Education degree from the University of Virginia. Mia has always had a passion for music since childhood and has traveled internationally, singing and performing. She spent a season in Rome, Italy, performing opera for the Opera Festival of Italy. Her first album, *Look Up*, was released in 2015, followed by her sophomore album, *No Days Off*, in 2018. In 2020, Mia released *Hark Medley*, a Christmas tribute. All proceeds from the tribute went to benefit Rebuild Haiti, a ministry to the Haitian people. In 2021, Mia's song titled *Abide* was released. This was her first endeavor writing for other artists. This year, Mia released her single entitled *Resurrection*, featuring her two oldest children, who co-wrote the project.

Mia has performed on the Nightline television show, was a featured artist for the Women of Purpose Radio Show, and was a featured artist at the Hampton Musician's Conference. She has taught vocal music in several schools, including the Young Musicians of Virginia. Mia Smith teaches women's Bible studies and youth bible classes for schools and churches. She is the founder of Mia Deneen LLC., which exists to help people get closer to God.

Instagram-Miadeneen
miadeneensongs@gmail.com

9

BETRAYAL OF MY INNOCENCE
Yvonnya Peoples

I used to be so excited about Saturdays; they were the best for me. I remember those childhood days in Douglass Park. Oh, how I loved it out there! Every Saturday was like a holiday for me because they were often filled with lots of fun. There was no school on Saturdays, and more significantly, I didn't have to get up super early. There were a lot of things I often looked forward to doing every Saturday, I could play my Atari game, Pac-Man, and I could definitely work those joysticks. I would watch karate flicks, trying to do some of the moves and chop something while getting ready to go outside with my friends. We especially liked playing on my friend's mom's school bus. We would take turns being the bus driver and doing what kids do to have fun.

Sundays were reserved for church, and I always looked

forward to singing in the choir. Being raised in the church didn't stop the evil one from invading my space. It started in 1981 when I was in the fourth grade. It was the same year as the attempted assassination of President Ronald Regan. Everything was in such chaos.

Moreover, it was a year that I would never forget, as it was the year a predator manifested in my life. I was betrayed by someone I trusted very much. Someone my family took as a family friend. Someone who was supposed to be a protector and have my best interest at heart. Never in a million years would I have expected to be harmed or hurt by this person in any form or fashion. Yet, this person was a secret predator, a deceiver to all. Everyone loved and admired him, but to me, he became my boogeyman! He was the nightmare I would carry for years, leading to my downward spiral and feelings of defeat.

No one knew I was being molested. When I was about 9 years old, I didn't understand what molestation was. I was just an innocent child who kept wondering what she did wrong. It started with one touch, then one stroke, and he kept going; I didn't know if I was supposed to like it or not. I thought he might stop, but he couldn't control his urges. He always took advantage of me at any opportunity he got. Thank God I wasn't alone a lot with him, but the little time he got almost ruined me for life. Now, he never penetrated me nor forcefully tried to have sexual intercourse with me. Yet he did enough to fulfill his sick fantasies. At first, I thought it was some type of game we were playing until I didn't like it, and his words were, "This is our secret; no one needs to know! Don't tell your mother." I can still remember the expression on his face as he said that to me. It was kind of spooky because now, we shared the same secret. What was I going to do? Who would I tell? Who would believe me? It was my word against this adult, and I didn't think I stood a chance.

So, my secret traveled through decades with me, well into my teenage years. I became promiscuous and had my first child at 15, then three more followed at 17, 19, and 21. My life was out of control. Trying to numb the pain, I became a heroin addict. Back and forth to jail and prison. See, a lot came with me keeping that secret. If only I had told someone what I was dealing with. I searched for love in all the wrong places until the day I was raped by 4 men and left in an abandoned house like trash. Maybe I deserved all of that, I had thought to myself. At that moment in my life, all I wanted was to die. Nothing seemed to be motivating me in life any longer, not even money. I was just a dressed-up junky. There was nothing I didn't do to escape this cruel world. But nothing worked; I still woke up daily and hated myself more.

Though it may seem like my life was a mess, there were times I had a good time, like when I was in the Girl Scouts, modern dance, and cheered for the Douglass Park Rams. Playing softball was fun, too; I also enjoyed playing the clarinet in school! My grades were good. I had a good upbringing during summer vacations with my family. I remember going to Busch Gardens, where we would have so much fun. Every summer, my aunt and cousins, my mom, and her only sister would come together to take us on vacation. One summer, we drove to Kings Dominion. Another vacation I enjoyed was visiting my Uncle Ben and his wife in Washington, D.C. We were a really close family. I never wanted for anything; my Mommy made sure of that. She didn't know the secret I had hidden so far within. I was afraid to share it because the boogeyman said it was our secret. As a result of the incidents, I became so rebellious, but it was my way of acting out. I just couldn't enjoy the good things anymore because deep down inside me, something was missing. My outlook on life changed. It's a pity that the world and the things of it can make your heart callous.

For many years, I ran and ran and hid that little girl that was violated. The girl who used to play with her Barbie Dolls, Easy Bake Oven and enjoyed getting the bowls after her mom made cakes! That little girl no longer existed. I was tormented in my mind by my past! It didn't help that it seemed to continue through obscene phone calls as if someone was trying to keep tabs on me, like a stalker.

I never went to any type of counseling or therapy or talked to anyone to understand the trauma that I went through and how it affected me. I kept my feelings hidden and bottled up on the inside.

I thought I was enjoying life to the fullest, going to parties, and being around people I thought were good for me. But I soon came to realize they were all jacked up like me; they were living a lie too. I could also see survival mode on them, making it easy for us to blend. It felt like we understood one another. My community of friends was dealers, addicts, thieves, etc. I liked the lifestyle, fast money, and a high that plateaued at its peak until there was no reaction from it anymore. When I overdosed, I thought my life would change and I would stop, but for only a brief moment, I could feel a calmness and stillness of peace. I just didn't know how to keep that peace that I was experiencing. I couldn't maintain it. Wow, I liked the warmth of it. I just didn't know it was Jesus with me the entire time. It would be years before I would experience the depth of His peace again, understand who it was with me, and realize why He didn't let me die in my sin.

I'll never forget the day my life changed forever. On April 19, 2010, I was visiting my probation officer, and my sister took me to see her. She wanted me to get my life together. I had picked up some felony charges and was about to be violated by my probation officer. I'm not stupid; I knew immediately what would occur next when she told me, "I'll send your next appointment to you in the mail!" I learned a warrant for my arrest would be issued, and without hesitation or delay, I bolted out of there! You would have thought I was Usain Bolt or something. My mind was made up. They're going to have to catch me like the gingerbread man. So, my sister stayed behind and reasoned with her. She told my sister about this program that I could go into that she believed could help me get on track.

I left them in the office and returned to what I was familiar with, putting a needle in my arm. Here's the game changer: I ended up at a friend's house in the bathroom, shooting dope into my veins and feeling my knees buckling. My heart started pounding fast. "THIS IS IT, Yvonnya, you're about to die!" I couldn't call on anyone in the house because no one knew what was happening in that bathroom but me! There was a battle going on, and it involved my life. I had one quick thought: to say, "Jesus," and that's what I did! The Word of God says, "Those who call on the name of Jesus shall be saved!" My Lord spared my life in that bathroom, and I was in disbelief. Then my phone rang, and it was my sister. "Where are you?" She asked. With hesitation, I asked, "Where are you?" "I'm still at the probation office, and we called Victory Gospel Chapel, and they have a bed for you," she replied. I was like, "She really doesn't know what just happened. She almost lost her sister."

My sister was so adamant about me not returning to prison that she stayed in that office until a breakthrough came to fruition. I get a little choked up whenever I remember that, even while writing this. To know His grace is to know the price He paid for me. Only by His grace am I here today, able to share with you how He has given me back my life, joy, and peace. My wholeness and wellness reside in Him! I'll never forget walking into that ministry in disbelief and saying, "Yvonnya, give it a try." I wasn't serious at first, but one day, I was sleeping after being there for at least a week. I heard these exact words spoken to me twice, though I wasn't sure the first time. I remember thinking someone was near and was the one who said something to me. I answered, "Who is in here?" I got no answer. I dosed back off and heard the words again. Here's what was spoken to me:

"Therefore if any man be in Christ, he is a new creature: old things are passed away; behold, all things become new." These are the words spoken to me by the Holy Spirit. I didn't know it was written in 2 Corinthians 5:17 KJV until it was shown to me by Evangelist Doris. I had been so shaken that I cried and told her what I heard, and she then took me to the word.

That day, my life changed forever instantly, and I was set free from the boogeyman, addictions, and self-hatred. I shared so much with Jesus like He didn't already know. I talked and laughed and cried until one day, there were no tears to shed. It wasn't a therapist; it was the wonderful counselor. I continued to rest in His presence, and to this day, I haven't stopped, and He keeps me going. Holy Spirit does what He was sent here to do: lead me into all truth and keep me growing in Christ Jesus my Lord! I don't have any regrets today. I forgave my perpetrator, the one who betrayed my innocence. I even prayed with him. Some would say, "How could you do that?" and I would simply say, "Forgiveness is essential to me maintaining my deliverance and healing." I was forgiven for my sins and all the not-so-pleasant things I've done in life before meeting Jesus.

"Whom the Son sets free is truly free indeed in Jesus" John 8:35 KJV.

My skeletons have been released to Jesus, and they can no longer torment me. I don't feel guilty or condemned; I'm liberated in Christ.

Today, I enjoy helping others to break barriers and strongholds which seem difficult to overcome, helping them to realize anything can be turned around, leading them from victim to victory! Be confident in who they are and know there is purpose in all they've been through. I help them to know they are more than a conqueror, and the pain they endured can push purpose in someone else!

I am helping others to come out of hiding, uncover what's been covered up, and be released from the cave of darkness. In Christ, we have come to crush the plans of the enemy. We will NO Longer Be Silent!

I am Tamar, and this is my story!

BIOGRAPHY
Yvonyya Peoples

Yvonnya Evans-Peoples is a minister, Christian Grief Coach Specialist, author, mentor, and motivational speaker. She is the Founder and Executive Director of Streets2Scripture Ministry and Build Me Up Sis, a ministry that builds women up and reinforces that they are loved no matter what has happened to them.

Born in the City of Suffolk and raised in Portsmouth, Virginia, she learned how to turn pain into purpose and trauma into triumph. Her tenacity helped her to fulfill the unique call on in her life. She is an intercessor for our people; she is a mighty warrior of God and operates in the office of the prophetic.

Minister Yvonnya has been featured on the 700 Club and is the author of "I Decree Encouragement," "Don't Be Discouraged', and currently working on her new book "From Streets 2 Scripture." She is also a co-author in the soon to be -to-be-released anthology, "I am Tamar-Come Out of Hiding," with the visionary Dr. Charlene D. Winley.

Affectionately called "Pastor Yvonnya" by those who love her, she works alongside her husband, Anthony Peoples, to build and develop "Men of Valor Evolving." Through her work in Streets2Scripture Ministry, she serves as a jail and prison liaison, reducing the likelihood of recidivism for formerly incarcerated men and women.

Pastor Yvonnya mentors, motivates, and educates young adults, helping them rebuild their character and self-esteem and find their identity in Christ. She is the mother of four beautiful daughters, grandmother of twelve, and resides in Portsmouth, Virginia, with her husband.

Facebook Yvonnya Peoples
Instagram
streets2scripture
streets2scriptureministry@gmail.com

10

CHOSEN
Lana Short

Abandonment...

According to my dear friend, Merriam-Webster, the word abandon means for one "to withdraw protection, support, or help from." The story of Tamar tells us that her father, King David, did, in fact, abandon her after her half-brother, Amnon, had raped and refused to marry her. As her king, David did nothing, but what made it even worse was that, as her father, he still did nothing to protect, support or help her. Similar to Tamar, my father abandoned me in a way as well. At least, that is what I believed for a very long time. This is the story of how a seven-year-old girl became stuck in a cave of guilt, shame, and grief, to resting in the subtle yet revolutionary fact that she was chosen and born for such a time as this.

From the time I was born, when you saw my dad, you would see me too; people even used to call me his shadow. I was the true definition of a daddy's girl and felt no shame in it whatsoever. Truth be told, I enjoyed every moment of it. Many would say that I was spoiled, but I would say, "I was blessed."

There was nothing that could tear us apart. Although I still can't remember the exact day that everything changed, I remember my mom sitting me down and telling me that my dad was sick and would have to stay in the hospital for a little while. From that day on, nothing was ever the same. He was in and out of the hospital and nursing homes, and we even had an in-home nurse stay with him during the day while I was at school and my mom was at work. We had just moved into our new house not even two years before his diagnosis when everything went haywire.

By the time I was seven, we had learned that my father had something called Early Onset Dementia at the age of 36. This disease atrophies the brain section by section, which means the brain is slowly deteriorating. As his illness progressed, his memory of me slowly faded away, and I will never forget the day my dad looked me in the eyes and had no idea who I was. Many people say I had to grieve twice, the day he transitioned, and the day I knew he had forgotten me forever.

As time went on, my mom and I would visit him every now and then, my mom more often than me. On one specific Father's Day, our church decided to have the service at my father's nursing home. Being that he was the church's assistant pastor that he and his best friend had started, I just knew he would love every bit of us all being together again, worshiping like old times. Not too far into the service, my father began to have a panic attack that would be one of the most traumatic things I had witnessed at the young age of ten. Seeing his reaction truly rocked me to my core, and on that day, I decided that I didn't want to visit him anymore, mainly because I was scared to see him like that. Still, I later realized that I blamed myself for his reaction and didn't want to be the cause of another outburst like that. I know… that's a lot for a ten-year-old to carry.

In February of 2012, it was the weekend before Valentine's Day, and my middle school was having a Valentine's Day dance that Friday after school. In the few days leading up to the dance, I begged my mom to let me go, but with my dad's time here on earth ending, my mom refused. However, my uncle convinced her that going would be a good thing considering everything that was happening. That weekend, my aunts were at our house to keep my mom company and provide support while I stayed at what I call my "other mother's" house. I can still remember how everyone kept trying to convince me to go see my dad because no one was really sure how much time he truly had left, but I stood firm on the decision I made those few years back and continued saying, "No." The morning after the dance, I just couldn't shake the feeling that I should go see him and tell him how much I love him and that everything would be okay. Now, I know that it was Holy Spirit who told me to go see my father for what would be the last time. After sitting with myself for a little bit, I left the room and asked my other mother if she could take me to see my dad.

When we arrived, I didn't know what to expect. Thinking

about it now, I don't think I was prepared for what I saw when I walked into that room. My aunts and cousin were there, but they immediately cleared the room so my mom, dad, and I could all be together one last time. He was hooked up to a machine that was breathing for him, and with every rise and fall of his chest, more tears fell from my eyes and down my face. The doctors said they were surprised that he lived as long as he did because he had already surpassed the life expectancy by about two or three years. Fifteen minutes after I had left the nursing home, my other mother's phone rang, and I already knew what was being said on the other end. My best friend had taken his last breath. It was as if he had waited for me and only for me to come back to see him knowing that it was okay for him to go. This moment later led me to blame myself for his long-suffering. If I had just gone to see him sooner, maybe he wouldn't have been in pain for so long.

As the years passed, the hole he left in my life grew bigger. I began to search for that love in all the wrong places. I was severely depressed, addicted to marijuana, and a liar in every form of the word; lust ruled my life, and with every wrong decision, I just pushed myself further and further into a cave of guilt, shame, and grief. Now, while my father didn't intentionally abandon me, that was how it felt inside, that my father withdrew his protection, support, and help. I later learned that my real anger wasn't directed at my earthly father at all, but at my Heavenly Father. I believed that my Heavenly Father withdrew His protection, support, and help by taking away the one person who was supposed to help guide and teach me. I felt He took away the one person who could just hold me for hours at a time until I realized that it would all be okay.

It wasn't until I was in high school that I heard Him say so softly, "I chose you." Of course, with me not being on cool terms with the head honcho (God), I ignored Him thinking, "Why would you choose me out of everyone in this world to lose my best friend, my father?" I later learned that what He meant was that He didn't choose me to lose my father, but He chose me to be His daughter and invited me into what the Bible calls "sonship." He chose me even when I didn't choose Him while lying to those I cared about. He chose me even when I was high out of my mind. He chose me when my lustful nature led me to be sexually assaulted by someone I thought I could trust by reminding me that I am fearfully and wonderfully made. He chose me by being the light not only at the end of my dark tunnel of depression but by being the quiet, soft voice inside of it with me, reminding me that yet what we suffer now is nothing compared to the glory He will reveal later. What I didn't know was that He was setting me up to be a living testimony of His grace and mercy.

For so long, I hid behind my circumstances and allowed myself to believe the lie that "it doesn't get any better than this."

During my sophomore year in college, I gave my life to

Christ, and He began to show me the why of it all. I learned about one of His many names, Jehovah Shammah, which means "The Lord is There." He began to show me every situation He kept me in and brought me through. He began to remind me why I couldn't go to certain places and why I was punished when I disobeyed. Was it really a punishment though, or was it a lesson in how important obeying and heeding His instruction is? One of the most incredible things about God is that the Word tells us that He uses it all for our good. For me, He used my father's death as an invitation to fill a void I thought would be there forever and welcomed me into sonship. He used my time hiding in my cave of guilt, shame, and grief as an incubator to learn what authentic agape love is. This is a love that will protect, support and help me for the rest of my days. I was chosen.

I am Tamar, and this is my story!

BIOGRAPHY
Lana Short

Lana Short, 23, was born and raised in Fairfax, Virginia. She is finishing her Bachelor's degree at Old Dominion University, where she is pursuing a major in Psychology and a minor in English, focusing on Creative Writing. She is also an intern with Write It Out Publishing LLC. Her writing journey begin began when she was just a child. Lana and her father used to make up bedtime stories together instead of reading the traditional ones we all had grown to love. Her passion for writing has continued to grow more and more, as well as her love for helping others. From a young age, she knew that she would always love to help and on to help support others in any way she could, whether by giving hugs, a helping hand, or a listening ear. Lana plans to one day become a family therapist and continue to expand her joy of writing by publishing her own works. This anthology is truly her coming-out story, and she is excited to help someone else through their journey of what it means to be chosen.

Facebook-Lana Short

11

I AM MELODY
Melody Sidberry

My name is Melody. I am the last of five children to a clinically depressed single mom. I was violated through sexual abuse, molestation, and incest by different individuals, which began during my formative years. By the time the sexual violation ended, I was 13 and nothing but a mess.

Violation: After being raped by her half-brother, Amnon, Tamar was further transgressed when Amnon immediately hated her. He threw her out of his place like a piece of trash. Like Tamar, my offender was mean to me. I grew up being teased by the offender in my home a lot. So, in addition to being abused sexually, I was the ugly, black, nappy-headed girl. When no positive adjectives are ascribed to you, then the negative ones you hear always win out. Like Tamar, there was no justice offered to either of us. Her brother was not held responsible for the crime he committed against her; likewise, neither was my abuser. The Bible tells us that after the violations, Tamar lived in her brother Absalom's house as a desolate woman. Unlike Tamar, I was a child and had nowhere to go. I was forced to stay in the same place where my Amnon and my King David lived. I was forced to sit at the same table and break bread with the same one who caused my stomach to hurt and my appetite to disappear. Unlike Tamar, who expressed opposition to what her half-brother wanted, I was sexualized so early in life that I didn't even know how big a crime it was. I was only eight when I realized that what was happening was wrong. Unlike Tamar, I was silent and in anguish, for there were no words to describe what had occurred, no vocabulary to express the betrayal, disrespect, disdain, and desecration that left me in a state of desolation.

Thank God for the finished works of the cross. At 14, I met Jesus. When you get saved, there is no clear-all button for all the muck and mire that reside in us as a result of sin. That evening, the minister said, "The devil is coming after you now that you have come into God's kingdom." What!!! Did I really need the devil coming after me? All was not well at church, and after the first encounter with church hurt, it would be decades before I renewed my relationship with God and the church. I did not feel as though I mattered to anyone. In hindsight, like Tamar, I expected my family to do something to alleviate the pain and anguish. I wanted someone in that house to help me. I wanted my abusers to stop what they were doing and be remorseful. I WANTED MY MOTHER to hold me and tell me it would be alright, that I didn't have to be afraid anymore. I wanted the nightmares to stop.

Oh! The losses that come from incest. The dictionary defines desolation with such synonyms as grimness, dismalness, emptiness, loneliness, and isolation. It's as though a spoke was placed in the wheel of my development. How do you do relationships in an environment where you have no value? The essential components of healthy development: trust, communication, nurturing, and safety, did not exist in our home. As a result, it would be decades before I would begin to heal.

Thoughts of suicide in elementary school faded as I began to stand on my mother's bed, Bible in hand, preaching to myself. That year my teacher wrote on my report card, Melody Has Potential. Not knowing what it meant, I began to study potential. I understood there was more to me than my dysfunctional beginning. A teen mom at 17 to a precious little one, I had no idea how to parent or ask for help. I want you to know that there is isolation, hopelessness, anguish, depression, arrested development, fear, and anxiety that takes in that place of desolation. But thanks be unto God that He gives us victory; He never leaves us alone. Wherever we find ourselves, He is there, even in the darkest places.

Statistics in this country say that 1 in 8 girls will be sexually assaulted in some form by the time she turns 18 years old. We often take to the streets angrily with placards to protest the killing and mistreatment of people of color. Yet, in our homes, the contemptuous treatment of our sacred girls goes unmentioned. If we want the good of all, then the chant "No Justice - No Peace" must begin to ring in our homes and communities. A simple definition of justice is -To make right. Whether the perpetrator is a parent, silent family member, relative, or friend, we have got to make it right. Every Tamar deserves justice.

We can reclaim our families and communities when we make it right. Mordecai told Queen Esther, "Do not think that because you are in the king's house, you alone of all the Jews will escape. For if you remain silent at this time, relief and deliverance for the Jews will arise from another place, but you and your father's family will perish." Esther 4:13-14 KJV. How many families have died from the malnourishment of silence? When you are silent, you can't speak life, and you can't encourage. Dr. Martin Luther King Jr said, "We begin to die when we are silent about the things that matter most." What matters most in a family? Is it, not each member? Is the dreams and the ability to dream dying when we are silent? I remember asking my mother what she wanted to be when she was a child, and her response was, "I didn't have no time for that. In this place of desolation, you will understand the possibility of children just trying to survive, as there is no room to dream of the future. Not every child can afford the luxury of dreaming." God help us!

Thank God for His promises of redemption, recovery, and restoration.

Initially, I was excited about writing this chapter. As I thought about the topic of incest, my excitement gradually dissipated. Writing about my life meant I would have to tell my family, who had no idea who Tamar was, and how her life paralleled mine. Thank God I was able to get excited again. See, I prayed in my living room some years ago, and God gave me a vision. In the vision, water was pouring from the ceiling. I had a flat grey plate with which I was trying to catch the water. Needless to say, I was running from one side to the other with the water still falling from the plate I held in my hand. The next thing I knew, five cups were on the floor, and the water went directly into each cup. When I had the vision, I looked up the meaning of numbers in the Bible. The number five symbolizes God's grace, goodness, and favor toward humans. There were five cups, five members of my immediate family, and even five letters in the words, "peace and grace." I thought about it for some time. Even today, God still manifests His providence in my life with this vision. At first, I felt

God was just trying to tell me not to worry. Yet more than that, to be at peace.

The Prince of Peace dwells in me. Over time, the Lord has demonstrated what His peace is. Often, therapists say to me, "How did you make it this far?" or "You really are a strong woman." I quote Phillipans 4:7, "And the peace of God, which passeth all understanding, shall keep your hearts and minds through Christ Jesus." KJV. It is God's peace when it doesn't seem like you are going to make it. When it looks like the situations and circumstances will overtake you, trust and believe that God is faithful and will guard your heart and mind.

I love that God loves us unconditionally. He doesn't want any to perish but that everyone would change their minds about Him. I know the guilt and shame associated with incest for all parties involved, which is the main reason for the secrecy. However, God forgives all sins, not just some. He comforts and gives peace. He restores you better than you were before. To the mother who is heartbroken and anguished by the violation that one of your children has bought upon another related child, Isaiah

61:1-4

To the child violated by relatives - Tell somebody else until someone will listen and act on your behalf and know that God is in the business of restoration. He promised to restore the time and your health. He makes all things new.

To the perpetrator of the violation, God loves you also; you are included in His plan. He can heal all and any afflictions. Give Him your shame, guilt, and embarrassment. There is room at the cross for you.

No longer alone, unwanted, neglected, or fearful.

Recently, I heard these words, by S. Kelley Harrell, from her book Gift of the Dreamtime, "Suffering happens in isolation, but healing happens in community." God never meant for us to go through this life alone. I thank Him for Dr. Charlene D. Winley and all the women in the Tamar Anthology and the Facebook Groups; Broken to Beautiful and Self Care is Soul Care.

It is a spiritual battle. There is real work to be done. We must do the work. Today, I stand as the woman God called me to be, Free. As I apply His truth to the lies I believed about myself, breaking the silence, renouncing soul ties, and walking in my identity in Christ, I am Free! Again, I'm Melody, and I've come out of hiding.

I write this chapter in honor of my mother and the many women who never had the freedom to realize their dreams and purposes. May God be glorified. It is my testimony that nobody but You, Lord, rescued me when I was in trouble, nobody but You, Lord.

I am Tamar, and this is my story!

BIOGRAPHY
Melody Sidberry

Melody Sidberry is a native New Yorker. She is the mother of two lovely daughters and the grandmother of three adorable grandchildren. After working 24 years as an Unit Clerk in the Inpatient Physical Rehabilitation Unit at Mount Sinai Hospital, she retired in 2021. For ten years, she served as an usher at Soul Saving Station for Every Nation Christ Crusaders of America, Inc, where she currently attends. She was an actively involved PTA member at Frederick Douglass Academy II. She volunteers as the Resident Council Member of the New York City Housing Authority. She is an avid reader and in her spare time, she enjoys decoupage crafting and writing.

Facebook-Melody Sidberry

12

TRAUMA TO TRIUMPH
Roz Caldwell Stanley

"He always comes alongside us to comfort us in every suffering so that we can come alongside those who are in any painful trial. We can bring them this same comfort that God has poured out upon us." 2 Corinthians 1:4 TPT

My mom was 17 years old when she gave birth to me; at the time, she was already married with a child. Before my birth, my dad joined the military to care for his family and stay out of trouble. Both were so young and ill-equipped to manage adulthood and family life in a mature and healthy manner. They were doing what they knew, saw, or improvising as they grew up. They survived, but my dad disappeared when I was around six. I remember visiting him once in prison.

Eventually, we had a different "daddy." He was a good provider, a strong, multitalented, and gifted man. Everyone was afraid and, at the same time, respectful of him. However, all his good characteristics changed when he started drinking; he became

mean and violent. Many years of my life were filled with his multi-

abusive nature. A day came when my mother, sister, and I had to

put him out by violent force. I didn't know the effects of abuse had

already set in, to be activated throughout life in unhealthy ways to

my unknowing. Fear, rejection, shame, self-protectiveness, trust

issues, self-reliance, workaholism, sexual promiscuity, and other

negatives were living in my soul. My soul had been wounded

without receiving the necessary treatment to bring about

wholeness. But who knew? I was functioning well. I was making

it. I was progressing (so it seemed on the outside).

Living in a home with domestic violence, an alcoholic

stepfather, being sexually and emotionally abused as a child,

becoming pregnant at age 12 by my gang leader boyfriend, who I

later learned was cheating on me and was a heroin addict, as well

as other trials, I realize now empowered me with the ability to be

used by God in the lives of others. These experiences helped me

see people in ways I cannot describe. They gave me a hunger to be

free and want others to be free. They gave me a passion for helping people heal and families be healthy! They helped to provide me with the ability to be slow at judging a book by its cover and be willing to investigate and read it, hoping to help bring it to a good ending! My empathy for others, regardless of their presentation, socioeconomic status, or ethnicity, was put into me!

As a single mom, after two divorces, my mom did her best to give her children a better life, a broadened outlook, and a desire to progress. Most of the time, she worked three jobs. With a GED, wherever she worked, favor worked for her, leading her into supervisory and management positions. This required me to take on a role in my household that was beyond my age. Along with already being a single mom as a child, helping to care for my younger siblings, and taking on household responsibilities while being a child, unbeknownst to me, disrupted years of natural emotional and mental growth and development. But who knew? I always thought that I was doing well. Like my mother, favor followed me too. Some of the quick learning gifts she had were passed on to me. However, life showed me that negative generational issues, unhealthy behavior patterns, harmful beliefs and thoughts, unresolved emotional pain, and unaddressed traumatic issues are also passed down.

So I followed in her footsteps. I got married young with a child. Eventually, I gave birth to a son. But internally, I was screaming, "I refuse to be poor! I refuse to stay in the hood! I refuse to let a man control my life! I refuse to stop at a high school education!" But I was a young woman without the proper training necessary to take on the things I was stepping into. But who knew? I was functioning. After a few years of marriage, I separated and divorced. I became, again, a single mom. However, my kids and I looked good. We appeared to be making it. And according to life without Christ, we were.

I had completed college, had a good job, belonged to a well-respected Baptist church, sent my children to a Christian school, and had even gone to a counselor attempting to address issues. However, I was also a party animal, a marijuana smoker, and involved in unmarried sex. One day, a spontaneous encounter with God through a Bible question/homework assignment that I was helping my children with caused me to immediately feel a need for more of God, along with a need to choose what I wanted

to present to my children as the proper lifestyle.

Not long afterward, a friend invited me to visit a different

church. While there, I felt something I had never felt as the

congregation stood praising God with a joy and enthusiasm I had

never experienced. The Pastor was teaching straight from the

Bible. When he ended his message, he began sharing what a

relationship with Jesus Christ looked like. My heart was drawn, my

soul was being massaged, and a hunger for this life rose in me.

When offered the opportunity to receive Jesus, my response was

immediate. As a matter of fact, I was so changed on the inside that

I immediately discontinued contrary behaviors. The most difficult

to let go of was my male friend and our sexual relationship.

Through prayer, including crying out to God for help and a

determination to live God's way by abstaining from sex, that

relationship eventually ended.

I soon learned about "the glory of virginity" and the

negative impacts that sexual involvement not aligned with God's

Word brings about. My first level of soul healing, particularly regarding sexual issues, came through "The Christian Men's Network," founded by Dr. Edwin Louis Cole (deceased). As he taught sex God's way, he began to talk about people who had been misused and abused sexually. He asked those in the room who had been sexually misused or abused and wanted to be healed to step out of silence for him to pray for them. The emotions in the room were high. I had never heard anyone talk about sex and sexual abuse so openly! As we began to stand, he looked at each of us one by one, in our eyes, men and women. All felt the intensity of the moment. He then began to repent to us individually, role-playing to be the ones who sexually misused or abused us, asking that we forgive him.

Forgiveness, the power of it, and the reason for it is more for the one forgiving than the one being forgiven. To separate you from the offender and the sin they committed against you so that you would no longer carry the burden. Other family members besides my stepfather had sexually misused and abused me. Through tears and sobs, I forgave... all of them. As he prayed for healing, I felt God's power upon me and a feeling of purity entering my being! I was free! It was amazing!

Eventually, I received the call of God to become a Christian counselor, and God led me to a Christian university requiring a major relocation. A few months before the relocation, I met a man at church who was kind, humble, and hungry for God. He was strong in the Word of God and serious about his relationship with God. We got along well. My children, friends, and family liked him. We began spending much time together, mostly surrounding church activities. I learned that he had been in prison for murder. He had admitted his wrong, repented, and did his time. He met Jesus while in prison and became a known Christian leader there. He was a good friend of two godly men I loved and trusted, so I had no qualms about his past indiscretions believing he was delivered and had become a new person.

After a late departure from a church picnic, instead of me driving him home, which was a 90-minute drive, we agreed that he would stay in my area since we would be going to church early the following day, which was closer to where he lived. We planned to ask one of the single men from our church who lived nearby to allow him to sleep on their sofa. However, it was so late by the time we arrived in my town, we decided not to, and he would sleep on my sofa. So after getting the children settled, I sat in the living room talking with him. At the beginning of our relationship, we both agreed that we wanted to maintain sexual abstinence until marriage which we maintained with no temptations.

This particular night, however, we began to kiss. Then we engaged in petting which went beyond our norm into sexual touching. When I realized the potential of our behavior, I disengaged, apologized for my part, stated that we needed to be careful, said good night, and went to my bedroom. My custom was not to close my bedroom door at night to always hear and be available to my children, which is what I did that night. Once I changed my clothing, I prayed as usual, turned out the light, and got in bed. I don't know how much time went by; I must have fallen asleep but was awakened by this man on top of me. My door was closed. I asked him to get off. I questioned what he was doing, reminding him of our agreement regarding sex. He began talking harshly and vulgarly, telling me to shut up, insisting I wanted this.

I tried to wiggle away, and he became violent, pinning me down and stripping off my clothes. I realized that this was a man who had committed murder. I remembered that my children were in the other rooms. I feared for my life and theirs, so I kept quiet while he raped me.

When he finished, he got up and returned to the living room. I didn't sleep. I was anxious for the morning to get him out of my house. Looking back, I realize that I was in shock. I didn't yell, scream, or make him leave. I just waited. When morning came, I awakened my children and followed our typical morning-before-church routine. That morning, anyone I told of what had happened the night before would have called me a liar because he had turned back to the kind, likable person we knew. But I knew differently. I drove us all to church. When he exited the car, I told him I never wanted to see him again.

This particular Sunday, our guest preacher was Dr. Edwin Louis Cole. As he was preaching, he hesitated and said, "I have to be obedient and follow the lead of the Holy Spirit." He looked in my direction. He said, "A woman in this church was raped last night. The man who raped her is in here, too. I don't want you to stand, but God is leading me to say to this lady, you are healed! God is healing you, and he will take care of him." As he spoke, a tingling sensation went through my body. It took everything in me to maintain my composure. Tears dropped from my eyes. I received those words as God stretched His arms of love out to me and surrounded me. I did tell my closest friends what happened. Once relocating for school, I engaged in counseling for my childhood and past issues. However, this rape did not impact me as it could have. God saw me! God healed me!

Being raped by a man who seemed to love God and others could have made me completely distrust men. It could have triggered me into a deep shame and blame myself. It could have kept me in a place of emotional pain and unforgiveness. It could have even kept me from going on to school. As my mom often said, 'But God....'" He made a way for me! Understanding forgiveness and repentance helped me quickly forgive that man, forgive myself, and repent for my wrong decision-making. And I did learn caution in relationships realizing that deep kissing and petting are dangerous to maintaining sexual abstinence before marriage. I also realized that, regardless, **he had no rights to my body and that the rape was not my fault.**

Through the privilege of being trained as a professional counselor, going through personal counseling, my relationship with God, and time spent with Him and in His Word, the Lord has taken me through soul healing. This has allowed me to be an avenue of healing to others (2 Corinthians 1:4). I maintained sexual abstinence for 15 years until marriage to my husband, Arthur.

However, meeting Jesus Christ as my Savior and Lord and receiving the soul healing that only He can provide... *It is by His stripes that we are healed* (Isaiah 53:5). This has anchored my hope and given me a deep knowing that people can be helped, people can change, and people can be healed! But if no one tells them if no one is sent to them..., how will they know? How will they get free from the emotional pain, the thoughts, the unresolved grief, the trauma, or the negative generational patterns that plague their lives!?

What happened to me has been turned into my empowerment to empower others' lives. That was then. This is now. I am grateful to be in a place of uplifting the lives of others!

I am Tamar, and this is my story!

The Passion Translation®. Retrieved April 15, 2023, from https://www.thepassiontranslation.com

BIOGRAPHY
Roz Caldwell Stanley

Roz Caldwell Stanley, a semi-retired Licensed Professional Pastoral Counselor, has provided professional people-helping services, consulting, training, and counseling for the past 30 years through various collaborations with other organizations and her own professional counseling service. She has written five books to help improve lives: *Soul Healing-For Such a Time as This; Prayers for Living: Prayers to Help You Get Through Life; Revolutionizing Families: Changing The Way You Live & Love; Stress Indication Test: An Informal Tool to Help Christians Reduce Stress; and African American Family Life: It's Time To Get It Back.*

Roz is the founder of *Healing of the Soul Ministry (ministry4soulhealing.com)* and the developer of the Healing of the Soul prayer counseling modality that leads people to healing & deliverance from soul wounds & traumas. She provides training for those desiring to become Healing of the Soul Ministry Certified Ministers, as well as speaking or providing emotional, spiritual, or relational well-being training sessions. Roz is also an adjunct professor at Tidewater Bible College in Virginia Beach, VA. She is the wife of Pastor Arthur Stanley. They are blessed to share 5 adult children (including 1 son in love) as a blended family, 12 grandchildren, 6 great-grandchildren and one on the way. Purchase her books at https://www.amazon.com/author/rozcaldwellstanley

Facebook-Roz Caldwell Stanley
IG-Rozbecauseofgrace

13

SMALL PACKAGE, BIG BENEFITS
Gloria J. Winley

In 1949, my father, the Late Bishop Jesse H. Winley, accepted Jesus Christ; a year later, he felt the call to preach. My parents took a train to Buffalo, New York, because God had called my father to go on a mission there. Just like every new believer, my father had a lot of concerns. He was concerned about my mother's reaction because, at the time, she was not yet a Christian. But God promised him that everything would be okay. My mother never challenged his decision or reacted negatively regarding his new belief; instead, she willingly followed my father's obedience to God.

Midway through the trip, my mom started crying. My father comforted her, asking whether the tears resulted from her leaving her familiar surroundings. She said, "No," but remained inconsolable because she couldn't see herself as a pastor's wife as she wasn't a Christian. My father prayed with my mother, and she accepted Christ on the train that day.

At the time of their transition to Buffalo, my mother was pregnant with me. I was my parents' fifth child and the firstborn on the mission field.

The Lord sent my parents to Buffalo so that they could learn faith, confidence, and trust in God. I recall my parents telling me that the housing authority in Buffalo did not have a plan in their construction to build a five-bedroom apartment to house our family. The Lord kept telling my father to keep going back and that He was in charge of city hall, and they did construct an apartment to fit my family. Many nights there was not enough food to eat, and the food would multiply as we ate. Frequently, my mother would boil water, and by the time the water boiled, somebody knocked on the door, telling my mother they were at the grocery store and picking something up, which would be our dinner. My family witnessed faith in action and watched the power of God move miraculously many times on our behalf. The Winley family, now twelve children, returned to New York City. After the passing of the founder, Bishop Billy Roberts, my father became the Bishop and General Overseer of the Soul Saving Station for Every Nation Christ Crusaders of America, Inc.

My parents did the work of the Lord and instilled a strong faith in Christ in their children at a young age. The church was the hub of my extracurricular activities. We filled gleaners with quarters to fund missions, conducted dramatizations, and had the youth sing at nursing homes and hospitals. We also had youth fellowship with different churches. It was second nature for me to give back because of the lessons I learned about serving. I also enjoyed sewing and had an eye for fashion; I loved matching different clothing items.

In high school, juniors and seniors could participate in federally supported work incentive programs that allowed them to work at age 16. I met the requirements to work at the Post Office and couldn't wait to seize this fantastic opportunity. I would put in 16 hours per week on weekends, and I was ecstatic. My father, however, did not share in my newfound happiness. He saw how neglecting my spiritual growth by a year of church absence would hurt me. I went against my father's desires and got a job. It turned out that I really liked it and that having my own money wasn't such a horrible idea, especially having eleven younger siblings. I thought it would be fantastic to have some independence. The church activities did, indeed, decrease.

One day during the summer of 1968, I was about 18 and was out with a friend when I saw an acquaintance riding by on a motorcycle and wanted to join him. I hitched a ride on the back of his motorcycle and had a blast. I gripped him tightly as we turned a corner, and he assured me nothing would happen. He tried to take the bend quickly but lost control and crashed into a car, throwing me off the bike. I was knocked unconscious, and when I regained consciousness, I was transported by police in a high-speed attempt to reach the nearest hospital. It was a fight to save my life. My father was listed as my next of kin at the hospital, so he was contacted when I arrived.

At the time, my father was attending his church's annual convention. He got a call from the emergency room telling him I had fallen off the motorcycle, hit my head, and was in a state of unconsciousness with facial lacerations. I spent a total of ten days in the hospital. I remember calling my father every day for ten days straight, crying, "Daddy, I want to come home." My father was constantly there and prayed for me.

During my convalescence, a friend came to visit after I left the hospital and asked me to hang out with her. Reluctant to leave the house, I went through five outfit changes before deciding on what to wear. We went to a bar near where we had once lived. Never having set foot in a bar, I stayed for fifteen minutes before heading home. Little did I know that my path that night would cross with the man who would eventually change my life trajectory.

He volunteered to drive me home. During the ride, he informed me that he was a photographer, acknowledged my fashion sense, and asked if I wanted to do any modeling. He handed me a card for his maintenance company. I was startled that a man who was thirteen years my senior showed interest in me. Stupidly, I believed I was unique. A year and a half later, in my childish desire for a happily-ever-after, I shocked my parents by telling them I was married. Eventually, I found out my husband's real name. I discovered he had two children, seven and nine years younger than me, from a marriage he had left fifteen years prior but was not divorced. Unbeknownst to me, his wife contacted my father and told him they were still legally married and that he had left them. Finding this out, I was devastated because I was in love and in an illegal marriage. My husband assured me that a marriage is automatically severed and ended if you haven't been there in ten years or more. I believed him and never questioned him.

My parents were obviously disappointed with me, but they never made me feel unloved or abandoned, nor stopped praying for me. The consequences of sin are real, and my parents taught me that. When I think of a successful marriage and family, I think of my parents. They never fought or used harsh language in front of their children. My parents routinely gathered their children together for prayer and Bible study. Those were very memorable times, my siblings would agree. We were taught that no matter what happens to us, we should never be angry with God because He is perfect and never makes mistakes. My parents never wavered in their faith or reliance on God's promises to save all their children.

God's kindness and mercy were like a constant breeze that accompanied me wherever I went. Despite my many mistakes, the

Lord kept drawing me back to Himself. The way of the transgressor was extremely challenging for me, and no amount of remorse, isolation, shame, or embarrassment helped. Because of my decisions, I felt every ache, grief, pain, and disappointment. Every time I tried to pin the blame on someone else, God would show me how wrong I was.

My pregnancy with my daughter was God's way of revealing to me how much I lacked and needed Him. I became so aware of Him spiritually, and while life was being formed in me naturally, little did I know a spiritual awakening was taking place within me. As my mother did for me, I wanted to raise my daughter to reverence and love God and have a strong faith and Christ-centered values. Throughout my pregnancy, I felt a gradual but steady emotional shift. The Bible's verse Psalms 23:1 KJV— *"The Lord is my Shepherd, I shall not want..."*—inspired me to start praying and reading the Bible more regularly.

The more I read the Bible, the more the voice in my ear reminded me that I needed God amplified and the hole in my heart filled. My heart was prepared to receive Jesus Christ as Lord and Savior on Palm Sunday, 1972. I'll never forget the moment my mother removed my three-month-old daughter from my arms as I walked down a side aisle, sobbing. I knelt, prayed, and asked Jesus to be my personal Savior. I place a great deal of significance on my spiritual birthday. My daughter hears the details of my redemption narrative every Palm Sunday. I made the proper decision this time and have made Christ the Lord of my life. My mind was resting, my spirit had peace, and my heart overflowed with love. This event marked the beginning of my faith in Christ. Philippians 1:6 KJV reads, *"Being confident of this very thing, he which hath begun a good work in you shall perform it until the day of Jesus Christ."*

My husband disapproved of my decision to devote my life to Christ. He felt I should have consulted with him first and gotten his approval. My husband informed me that I only had one true friend because all of my girlfriends were his girlfriends, and he slept with all except one. He failed to see that my choice was unrelated to his feelings. His misunderstanding further muddied our already complex situation, and the marriage ended.

Since I committed my life to God, my friends gradually drifted apart because they no longer found me entertaining. Years later, God showed me the value of a Christian friend who prayed for me and repeatedly reached out to say "Hello." For years, I didn't respond. The influence of that friend continues to this day. God gave me a darling little bundle of joy in the form of a daughter, and I am honored to have raised her with a strong faith in Christ. God has blessed me with six grandchildren, the eldest of whom has gone to be with the Lord, and five great-grandchildren; they are the beauty that comes from the ashes. Every day, I ask God to help my grandchildren keep Christ at the center of their lives despite the many challenges they will face. I am the curse-breaker, foundation-maker, and repairer of the breach of my legacy (Isaiah 58:12 KJV).

I will no longer keep my story a secret and am no longer afraid to share it.

I am Tamar, and this is my story!

BIOGRAPHY
Gloria J. Winley

Gloria J. Winley is a mother, grandmother, community leader, servant, and woman of God. She grew up with 11 younger brothers and 5 sisters and naturally developed a nurturing spirit and a deep sense of responsibility for the well-being of others. Gloria's heart for service extended beyond her local community as she embarked on numerous mission trips to Haiti, Germany, Italy, Amsterdam, and London. Witnessing the transformative power of God's love expressed through the universal language of compassion and care, Gloria experienced firsthand the profound impact that faith can have on people's lives.

Gloria's law enforcement career began in her role as a Police Administrative Aide, and soon after passed the requirements to become a Police Officer. After an illustrious 24-year career with the elite New York City Police Department, Detective Gloria retired with a wealth of experiences and achievements.

Gloria's journey has been enriched by her commitment to deepening her spiritual knowledge and ministry involvement. She served as a Christian Worker and holds credentials from the Collegiate Bible Institute, serving as a Licensed Missionary, Licensed, and Ordained Evangelist at The Soul Saving Station for Every Nation, Christ Crusaders of America. Beyond her spiritual and professional endeavors, Gloria volunteered at the St. Albans Veterans Administration Medical Center Palliative Care. She is an esteemed lifetime member of the National Council of Negro Women (NCNW), serving as a board member and the Chaplain of the Queens County Section. Additionally, she is Health, Community Service and Youth Mentor committees. She is the recipient of President Biden's Lifetime Achievement Award, honoring her exceptional dedication and impact on the community.

Gloria remains steadfast in sharing the good news of the Gospel of Jesus Christ with all she encounters. Her life is a testament to the power of faith, the importance of service, and the transformative nature of love.

Facebook-Gloria J Winley
Glojwinley @aol.com

14

THE AFTERMATH
Dr. Charlene D. Winley

As we read, a trap was set, as it is frequently with victims of sexual abuse and molestation. It isn't something that just happens. It starts as a thought or conception in the mind, which leads to the act of violence and seeks to destroy your purpose and destiny.

Tamar knew the grave consequences of the violent, barbaric act upon her.

1. She pleaded her case-

2. This kind of thing is not done in Israel

3. Where will I show my face

4. You, Amnon, will be out on the street in disgrace

5. Ask father for my hand in marriage (even though she's about to be raped by Amnon, she is willing to marry him).

6. Nope- Amnon wanted it then and right now.

7. She pleaded against this atrocious action once his "lust," not love, was fulfilled; he despised and hated her.

Because the aftermath of the act would be worse than the rape itself. It is important to note that an all-consuming passion, lust, desire, "God, I got to have him or even her," should not be confused with love. For after Amnon satisfied his sinful lust, he despised Tamar. As stated earlier, his hatred after was greater than the "feeling of love" he felt for her. He wanted nothing to do with her.

Here it is where most women of abuse and rape are stuck. It matters not how long in years or the intensity of the acts of violence, strongholds, and confusion in the heart and mind are the results.

In the AFTERMATH

You're stuck in the aftermath after the storm hits, and there is a lot of devastation, clean-up, debris, destruction, and loss of lives. Women have responded differently to their afflictions and have taken various identities in response to their trauma. Without therapy, inner healing and deliverance, and counseling, you will continue to live your life from that point of trauma. You will be tied up and locked into a new pattern of behavior as the trauma has rewired your brain and created new neural pathways for making sense of your world. Even long after the memories fade away or in your feeble attempt to suppress them, "Your Body Keeps the Score," as author Bessel A. Van der Kolk mentions in her book.

In the aftermath of sexual trauma, you may have an insatiable or sexually perverted appetite. Often sexual trauma sexualizes children at an early age and plants seeds that will later reproduce in their teens. The root system has already been established, and it will take on a life of its own if not dealt it. From these faulty relationships developed, the inability to establish or maintain appropriate relationships will be a norm, and the cycle of trauma will continue to reproduce in a person's lifetime.

Then there are manifestations outside of sex. For example, the lack of boundaries will cause a person to manipulate and seek to control situations and/or people. On the other hand, people will manipulate and control you because the breach has never been repaired, and you are an open portal. You may lack emotional control, with emotions and thoughts oscillating from depression, anxiety, and unworthiness to despair and suicidal ideation.

No scripture in the Bible tells you to cope, deal with it, or get over it. The Word said He came to deliver and set the captives free. In the book's next section, you will read the stories of a few women who shared the stories of their traumatic events and how they processed through it, unmuzzled, and gained their voices back.

ABOUT THE VISIONARY

Dr. Charlene D. Winley is "The Soul Care Coach," a certified life coach, speaker, author, CEO, and founder of ReScriptedLife Coaching. ReScriptedLife Academy, and The Soul Care Series. Additionally, she is the visionary behind the SOON TO BE RELEASED anthology, "I am Tamar- Come out of Hiding! Through her own experiences of sexual mental abuse, homelessness, divorce, rejection, and grief, Dr. Winley equips EMPOWER professional women to rewrite the story of their life, by helping them to come out of hiding, recover their identity, and live their life by design and not by default. She speaks on trauma as related to physical, emotional, and sexual abuse, identity, soul care, and purpose.

Dr. Winley's reach is within the educational, religious, coaching, and trauma industry. Through the Soul Care Series, Dr. Winley uses her voice to empower women through quarterly transformational live weekly sessions. These sessions are geared to help women uncover hidden wounds, recover their identity, discover their purpose, and be activated in their calling.

Dr. Winley has a Master's degree in Human Development, Cognition, and Learning from Columbia University with a concentration in Clinical Psychology. She holds a doctoral degree in Educational Leadership from Nova Southeastern University in Florida. She is the vice president on the board of the Attachment Trauma Network, a driving force to promote healing of children impacted by trauma through supporting their families, schools, and communities.

Dr. Winley is a 5x times Amazon best-selling and international author. She published her first book, "ReScriptedLife-31 Days to Reconnect with Your Purpose," and the visionary of the newly released anthology, "I am Tamar- Come Out of Hiding." Dr. Winley co-authored 4 books, SurvivingHer-Count it All Joy, "God-Fident: Stories of Unshakable Faith," My Sister Helped Me Healed-The Power of Kingdom Sisterhood, and Surviving Her-The Art of Forgiveness.

Dr. Winley, a native New Yorker, is the mother of three sons, and currently lives in Virginia Beach.

Website www.charlenedwinley.com
Facebook Page-Dr. Charlene D. Winley
Instagram-drcharlenedwinley
Fb Group- Soul Care is Self Care
Email drwinley@charlenedwinley.com

REFERENCES

All Scripture quotations are taken from *THE MESSAGE*, copyright ©1993, 2002, 2018 by Eugene H. Peterson. Used by permission of NavPress. All rights reserved. Represented by Tyndale House Publishers, Inc.

The KJV is public domain in the United States. https://www.biblegateway.com/versions/King-James-Version-KJV-Bible/

Brenner, A. *Tamar and the coat of many colors. Samuel and Kings, A Feminist Companion to the Bible*, ed. (Sheffield: Sheffield Academic Press, 2000) 2/7:65-83 {page 65-83}

Fletcher, Elizabeth. *Women in the Bible.* ***www.womeninthebible.net.*** **Retrieved October 15, 2012**, from http://christianselfstudy.com/moodle/mod/page/view.php?id=220. © Accentuate. All Rights Reserved.

https://womeninthebible.net/women-bible-old-new-testaments/maacah-ii/
https://womeninthebible.net/women-bible-old-new-testaments/tamar-judah/tamar-amnon/
https://womeninthebible.net/women-bible-old-new-testaments/maacah-davids-wife/

God has smiled on me. Retrieved May 13, 2023, from https://www.lyricsondemand.com/r/revjamesclevelandlyrics/godhassmiledonmelyrics.html

Kadari, Tamar. "Maacah, the wife of David: Midrash and Aggadah." *Jewish Women: A Comprehensive Historical Encyclopedia*. March 1, 2009. Jewish Women's Archive. (Viewed on July 24, 2013)

http://jwa.org/encyclopedia/article/maacah-wife-of-david-midrash-and-aggadah>.

I want Jesus to walk with me. Retrieved May 13, 2023, from https://christianmusicandhymns.com/2022/10/i-want-jesus-to-walk-with-me.html

Mary Mack. (2023, March 11). In *Wikipedia.* https://en.wikipedia.org/wiki/Mary_Mack

RESOURCES

National Alliance on Mental Illness (NAMI) The NAMI HelpLine can be reached Monday through Friday, 10 a.m. – 10 p.m., ET. Call 1-800-950-NAMI (6264), text "HelpLine" to 62640 or email us at helpline@nami.org

National Domestic Violence Hotline: Domestic Violence Support. Call 800-799-7233 https://www.thehotline.org/get-help/

National Suicide Prevention Lifeline. 988 Suicide & Crisis Lifeline Call 988

We can all help prevent suicide. The Lifeline provides 24/7, free and confidential support for people in distress, prevention and crisis resources for you or your loved ones, and best practices for professionals in the United States. https://988lifeline.org/talk-to-someone-now/

Rape, Abuse & Incest National Network (RAINN) is the nation's largest anti-sexual violence organization. RAINN created and operates the National Sexual Assault Hotline 800.656.HOPE.

https://www.rainn.org/resources

Substance Abuse and Mental Health Services Administration (SAMHSA)

988 Suicide & Crisis Lifeline Call 988
SAMHSA's National Helpline is a free, confidential, 24/7, 365-day-a-year treatment referral and information service (in English and Spanish) for individuals and families facing mental and/or substance use disorders. https://www.samhsa.gov/find-help/national-helpline

Made in the USA
Middletown, DE
04 June 2023

31765884R00093